BATTLE UNDER THE MOON

BATTLE UNDER
THE MOON

An Account of the RAF Raid
on Mailly-le-Camp, May 3/4 1944

by

Jack Currie

Air Data Publications

Battle Under The Moon

First published in 1995
by AirData Publications Limited

Jack Currie is hereby identified as author
of this work in accordance with Section 77
of the Copyright, Designs and Patents Act 1988
A CIP record for this book
is available from the British Library

Printed in England by Redwood Books, Trowbridge

ISBN 0 85979 109 2

Illustrations by Lynn Williams

AirData Publications Limited
Southside, Manchester Airport,
Wilmslow, Cheshire. SK9 4LL

Contents

Foreword

'... the bombers, climbing out of Elsham Wolds, Killingholme and Kirmington, began to fill the sky with sound - enough to make a window rattle in its ageing mortar. Cassidy it was who voiced the query in our minds. "I wonder where they're going tonight."
"French target, for a dollar," said Cameron. "They mostly are, these days."
"Yeah, and they only count a third of an op," Knight added. "The blokes at Binbrook were really going crook about it when we were over there, eh, Bill?"
"Were they ever!"
"Then they went to - whaddya call it - Mailly-le-Camp ..."
"And lost forty-two, out of three-fifty odd ..."'

That's a snippet from "Mosquito Victory" - a book I wrote some years ago about the air war as it was in 1944 and 1945. The name of the target came up again at RAF Coningsby, when I was gazing at the Battle of Britain Memorial Flight Lancaster with the usual nostalgia. One of the ex-aircrew men who were showing people round came over for a chat, and it turned out that he had been shot down over Mailly-le-Camp. Some of the things he said about the operation made me want to find out more about it.

Almost immediately, came two strokes of luck: first, it transpired that the late Arthur Lee, co-founder of the Wickenby Register (Wickenby was the base of the squadron I first served with), had intended to write a pamphlet about Wickenby's part in the attack, and the Register's researcher, Jim MacDonald, had collected some material, which he passed to me; second, Martin Middlebrook, the author, who had produced an article about the operation some years earlier, made me free of his research. Then, with the help of the 44 Squadron Association, and more from the Wickenby Register, the word was spread along the old bomber-boys' grapevine that the story was being put together. Personal accounts came in, not only from this country, but from Canada, Australia, the USA and Europe, and I am grateful for the contributions all those people made.

Special gratitude is due to those who gave me leave to quote from their own documents, some published, others not. Among these are Group Captain Laurence Deane, DSO DFC, Mr. Andreas P. Moldt, DFM, of Denmark, Mr. Mike Allen, DFC, of Houston, Texas, Mrs. Crighton (Jack's widow), Mr. Greg Biefer of Nepean, Ontario, Mr. John Ackroyd of Dewsbury and Lieutenant Colonel Lionel Lacey-Johnson, the younger brother of a 101 Squadron navigator who gave his life in the course of the operation. A further debt is owed to the late Mr. Jim Carpenter, then Chairman of the Air Gunners' Association, who, for a reason which will emerge, had a deep and lasting interest in the fate of a 192 Squadron Halifax crew.

Mr. Terry Hanley and his wife Angie, of Tollerton, North Yorkshire, with Mr. Tony Scott as interpreter, undertook the research in France without which the story would not have been complete.

Lastly, my thanks go to the late Group Captain the Lord Cheshire, VC OM DSO DFC, who, in the midst of all his great endeavours for the welfare of others, found the time to give his encouragement and help.

Jack Currie, Easingwold, 1995

PUBLISHER'S ACKNOWLEDGEMENT

The Publisher would like to acknowledge the assistance given by Messieurs Bertin and Le Nours of the *Association Mailly* in the provision of some of the photographs in this book, and for permission to use part of their own publication, ***Objectif Mailly-le-Camp***, as reprinted in the Appendix.

CHAPTER ONE

TARGET MAILLY-LE-CAMP

Towards the end of April 1944, in the flat, green fields of the Champagne country between the courses of the rivers Marne and Aube, two farm labourers were cycling home to supper. The evening air was still as they approached their village, the silence only broken by the chirruping of birds in the hedgerows and the creaking of a rusty spring in Jean-Paul's saddle. They heard the growl of the engines and the rumble of the caterpillar-tracks long before the German tanks came into view.

Ahead of the column, a steel-helmeted motor-cyclist waved the Frenchmen off the road. Obediently, they dismounted, and propped their bicycles against the near-side hedge. They noted that the symbol, stencilled in yellow on the dull, grey paintwork of the leading Tiger's armour-plating, showed a letter "D" with a bar across the centre. Georges began to roll a cigarette. "Since we have nothing better to do," he said, "I'll count the tanks."

"Then, to occupy myself," said Jean-Paul, "I'll count the trucks."

The tanks thundered by, followed by a mixed fleet of armoured personnel carriers and heavy lorries. One of the tank commanders, standing in his turret, raised a hand and smiled at the Frenchmen, who affected not to see him. They watched while the head of the column passed through the village and turned into the gates of the military camp - the great training site which had been used by the French Army since the first World War, and by the Wehrmacht since the fall of France. It affronted Georges and Jean-Paul (who, as it happened, were both in the Resistance) that the Boches were in control, not only of the camp, but also of their village - and, indeed, of La Belle France. It was a terrible thing to be defeated in battle, and a shameful thing to be under occupation. Sometimes they blamed Marshal Pétain for all that had happened since 1940, sometimes Monsieur Maginot, sometimes Pierre Laval; sometimes they cursed the British, who had left France to the Boches - although not, perhaps, for very much longer, if what they heard was true.

When the column's rearguard of armoured cars had passed, Georges and Jean-Paul compared their calculations and rode on to the village. The name of the village was Mailly-le-Camp.

Three-hundred miles away, at a bomber-base in Lincolnshire, an RAF Wing Commander was tackling the pile of paper-work that had accumulated in his office while he and his squadron crews had been enjoying a few days' leave. He was a slender, dark-haired man, twenty-five years old, with a pale, clean-shaven face and wide-set eyes beneath thick, black eyebrows. If you had failed to notice the ribbons of the Distinguished Service Order and the Distinguished Flying Cross on his tunic and the occasional, involuntary tic in the skin beside one of those dark eyes, you could have taken him for an earnest young barrister, studying a brief - as he probably would have been, if not for Hitler's war. He was, in fact, one of the RAF's most experienced and successful bomber pilots, and he meant to go on flying until the war was won. A year ago, the Air Ministry had given him Group Captain rank (he had been, at that time, the youngest to achieve it) and a training unit to command but, as soon as he could with propriety, he had relinquished both the rank and the unit to return to operations. His name was Leonard Cheshire; the Squadron he led was No. 617 - known as the Dam-Busters.

Despite the paper-work, he was in good spirits: at last his theories about low-level target-marking had been accepted in the higher reaches of command. The AOC No. 5 Group, Air Vice-Marshal the Honourable Ralph Cochrane, had soon become his champion, and had argued Cheshire's case with the C.-in-C. himself. Air Chief Marshal Harris wasn't the most receptive of commanders to a newfangled notion, but he was a good judge of men and open to persuasion by results. He trusted Cochrane, and the results spoke for themselves.

Once the C.-in-C. had been convinced, there were no half-measures: much to his chagrin, the No. 8 Group Commander, Air Vice-Marshal Donald Bennett, had been ordered to give Cochrane three Pathfinder squadrons: No. 627, equipped with Mosquitos - the fastest twin piston-engined warplane in the world - and Nos. 83 and 97 Lancaster squadrons, which Bennett had originally obtained from 5 Group in 1942 to expand the nucleus of his embryo force. Not only that, but 617's Lancasters had been reinforced by six more Mosquitos, which the pick of Cheshire's Lancaster pilots had quickly learned to fly and, as quickly, had taken to their hearts. During the last few weeks, 5 Group's Mosquito crews had marked Brunswick and Munich for the heavies with devastating effect: they had hit marshalling yards and factories in France with the sort of pin-point accuracy which was needed if civilian casualties were to be minimised and which, although always striven for, had seldom been achieved - indeed, had never been the main requirement - on the city targets. Now, however, Operation "Overlord" lay ahead, and the allied bomber fleets were committed to preparing a way through Europe for Eisenhower's armies. There would be many targets in friendly countries under German occupation where inaccuracy, in the marking or the bombing, could cause the death of people who did not deserve to die.

The leader of the Resistance group to which Georges and Jean-Paul belonged was known to them as Reynard, although that was not his name. He studied their reports, compared them with others, and decided that someone in London ought to be informed. He wrote out a message on the back of an envelope, revised it several times until he had reduced it to the minimum of characters, and wrote it out again on a square of toilet paper. Having burnt the envelope and rolled the toilet paper into a ball which, in an emergency, he could bring himself to swallow, he set off on his bicycle to the lonely farmhouse where that rare animal, a French-speaking Englishman, shared a loft above the barn with a radio transmitter.

In London, the signal was decoded and passed to Intelligence. "According to our friends," wrote the assessing officer, "there has been a significant movement of medium tanks and support vehicles into the erstwhile French Army training depot at Mailly-le-Camp (map reference 4839N 0413E). From this report and others, and from recent aerial photographic evidence, it appears that the depot currently accommodates the 21st Panzer Divisional HQ, 3 Panzer Battalions, and elements of two more Battalions, probably recently withdrawn from the enemy's eastern front. The depot, which lies immediately to the east of Mailly-le-Camp village, comprises MT buildings and workshops, a tank training ground, a firing range and barrack accommodation for approximately 5,000 troops. Our opinion is that the depot, in addition to its training role, is intended to provide a reinforcement base for armoured operations in the event of an Allied landing in France."

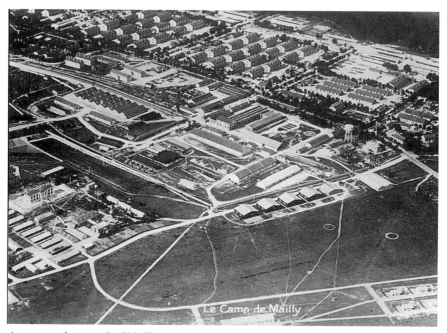

A pre-war photograph of Mailly-le-Camp.

The Intelligence assessment was passed to that sub-committee of the Chiefs-of-Staffs' Committee which dealt with candidates for aerial attack - their feasibility, significance and degree of importance. "We like the look of this one east of Paris," said the military representative. "Priority one, I should think. The more of their Panzer troops we can knock out, the better our chances when we cross the ditch."

"Very well," said the chairman who, in the Wonderland way in which Whitehall sometimes chose to work, was a civilian from the Research &

Experiments Department of the Ministry of Home Security. "It appears to call for a precision daylight raid. One for your B17s, eh, Colonel?"

The USAAF liaison officer nodded. "I guess so. We're kind of fully committed to airfields and transportation type targets right now, Chairman, as you know, but we'll get around to it in due order."

The Wing Commander representing Bomber Command raised a hand. "Perhaps we can help. I've no doubt the lads would appreciate a nice, quiet French target after - let's see - Cologne, Düsseldorf, Friedrichshafen and Essen in the last few days." He was careful not to catch the USAAF Colonel's eye, but he hoped the point was made: Bomber Command was destroying Hitler's heavy industry, while General Spaatz's bombers, apart from one or two recent ventures to Berlin, were flirting - quite capably, of course - but only flirting with the fringe.

The chairman raised his eyebrows. "Thank you for that, Wing Commander, but if I read the map correctly, this depot is only about a mile from the village of - what's it called?"

The secretary looked up. "I think it's pronounced 'Mah-eh-yee le Kahng', Chairman."

"Yes, Maylee-lee-Camp," said the chairman, sturdily. "Would the RAF be proposing a daylight operation?"

The Wing Commander smoothed his full moustache with the knuckle of a forefinger. "No, we would go by night, and preferably in moon-light. Have no fear, Chairman. I think we can claim a fair degree of accuracy - when it's required of us - and the target's just within range of our Oboe, which, as you know, is the most accurate radar bombing system in the world."

The USAAF Colonel smiled. "Too bad you don't have a bomb-sight to match it." The Wing Commander was searching for a suitable reply when the Chairman directed attention to the next agenda item.

The military depot at Mailly-le-Camp was included in the list which was passed to Bomber Command HQ, and there, in "The Hole" at Naphill, outside High Wycombe in Buckinghamshire, the Operations staff examined it with care. By this stage of the bomber war, the rules about how much force was needed to produce a given effect had developed from the realms of guess-work to the status of a science. If you told the professors in the back-room where and what the target was, they could say how many tons of high explosive would be needed to destroy it and, in arriving at this sum, they would have allowed for technical malfunctions, errors of judgement by the aircrews and the impact of the enemy. Although the total area of the depot was some nine square miles, most of it consisted of training ground in open fields, and the targets for the bombers - the administrative, technical and domestic sites - were confined to a comparatively small area. The weapon calculation for Mailly-le-Camp indicated a requirement for no more than two or three hundred tons of high explosive, an effort within the resources of four or, at most, five heavy bomber squadrons.

Under Air Chief Marshal Harris, however, the Operations staff never shrank from over-kill: they decided to commit an entire bomber group to the attack, and everyone knew which group that had to be. Early in the war the C.-in-C. himself (then an Air Vice-Marshal) had commanded No. 5 Group and, although he was a fair man in the general way of life, he was only human, and it was not unknown for him to bestow a certain patronage on those who had his favour. When, a month ago, he had ordered the hand-over of the Pathfinder Squadrons to the present group commander, he had also awarded No. 5 Group a measure of autonomy: Air Vice-Marshal Cochrane now had authority to evolve his own tactics and to mark his own targets.

Among the rest of the Command there was never any doubt as to who the blue-eyed boys were for the man they called "Butch" Harris. When a 1 Group pilot, in an idle moment, mused "I wonder who Princess Elizabeth will marry," another in the crew room was quick to answer: "I don't know, but I bet it's somebody from 5 Group." Mailly-le-Camp, it was decided at High Wycombe, would in all essentials be a 5 Group operation. Don Bennett's 8 Group would merely be required to provide a few Mosquitos, which would beam in on "Oboe" and illuminate the target area for Cochrane's low-level marker force. As for the date, the Command Met. Office gave a favourable forecast for the night of 3rd/4th May: the skies should be clear, with good visibility and a three-quarter moon. The target information was despatched to No. 5 Group Headquarters.

There, at St. Vincent's, a fine, three-storeyed building on the high ground east of Grantham, teleprinters clattered and telephones rang; Air Vice-Marshal Cochrane was appraised of the requirement. What happened next remains a minor mystery - not by any means the last in the story of the mission. It seems that Ralph Cochrane, having consulted his Senior Air Staff Officer and possibly his stars, decided to call for reinforcements. He picked up the green scrambler telephone and put a call through to Bawtry Hall, the yet more splendid mansion, forty miles further up the Great North Road, which served Air Vice-Marshal Rice, the Air Officer Commanding No. 1 Group, as a headquarters.

Although Cochrane and Rice maintained a cordial personal relationship, as did the other bomber group commanders, one with another, it has to be recorded that in career matters an element of rivalry occasionally crept in, rather as it used to six centuries earlier among the feudal barons, each of whom would loyally serve his monarch and hob-nob with his peers, but would gladly slit their throats to obtain a greater castle, a bigger band of bowmen or a more effective method of pouring boiling oil. It was in something of this spirit that Cochrane had acquired his own Pathfinder force, and in which Rice was doing his best to follow suit. Not having quite the same clout as Baron Cochrane of Grantham, however, Baron Rice of Bawtry could not plunder Baron Bennett of Huntingdon, and had been obliged to make do with what he had. From his own squadrons, therefore, in the previous month, he had formed a small target-marking force of six Lancasters, which were based at Binbrook as the "Special Duty Flight", under the command of Squadron Leader Breakspear, late of 100 Squadron. The fact that the unit had as yet made no great impact on the conduct of the war was no fault of its aircrews, for their chances to do so had been relatively few. On 1 Group's most recent operation, only two nights ago, they had marked a motor plant at Venisseux, near Lyons. The skies had been clear and there was no opposition. Flying Officer Maxwell of 12 Squadron, had been detailed to make a "special recce report" - a task which fell to most experienced captains at one time or another. "The SD Flight," Maxwell had reported, "seemed to find difficulty in accurate marking. The first phase aircraft had to orbit the assembly-point. The first TIs were scattered and the early bombing undershot."

Maxwell's strictures notwithstanding, the attack was quite successful; nevertheless, the SD Flight had yet to prove itself, and Air Vice-Marshal Rice was eager that it should. Not entirely unaware of this, Cochrane made his offer: "I'd be glad if you'd come in on this one with us, Winkel. Two waves on the depot buildings, my Group first, yours second. 'Goodwood' strength. All right so far?"

"Well, I'll talk to my people..."

"Then there are the tank repair shops - what I call the special target. Very important, apparently. I suggest you take that on yourself. A couple of squadrons, perhaps, and your SD Flight to mark it. What do you think?"

Why Cochrane made the offer will never now be known; that Rice could not refuse it is not hard to understand; that, in the aftermath, he would bitterly regret it, is known to be the case.

"Goodwood" strength meant that the heavy squadrons - apart from No. 617, whose activities, since the dam-busting raid, had been deliberately restricted to the sort of operations which called for special treatment - would put every serviceable aircraft on the Battle Order.

It is worth noting at this point that, in addition to the forecast of the weight of bombs required, the operational researchers could estimate how many bombers were likely to be lost on any given operation, and it was on the basis of this actuarial assessment that Command HQ, a few weeks earlier, had decided to relate the location of the target to the number of missions in a bomber crewman's tour. The decision was arbitrary: a successful flight to a target inside the German borders counted as one completed operation: those to targets outside, in the occupied countries, only rated as a third. It was not an entirely popular conception: for newly-trained crews, ready - even eager - to embark upon a tour of what they expected to be thirty operations, to be faced instead with a possible ninety, albeit not of quite so hazardous a nature, was a slightly daunting prospect; for experienced crews with, say, three or four missions to fly before their "screening", to find their tours extended by another nine or twelve was quite a blow. Nevertheless, that was to be the rule, and Mailly-le-Camp was 130 miles short of the nearest German border.

There was a number of bomber men to whom the one-third rule couldn't matter less - it made no difference to the tenor of their ways. They didn't see their operational careers in terms of numbers, and probably couldn't tell you, without checking in their log-books, exactly how many missions they had flown. Their spirit led them to go on and on, until someone called a halt - some M.O. perhaps, who, noticing the symptoms of extreme fatigue, the pallor, the tremor, the occasional instance of irrational behaviour, would have a word with the C.O. and arrange for the man to be "screened" from operations for a while, if not for good. In all the aircrew trades - pilots, navigators, bomb-aimers, wireless-operators, flight-engineers and air gunners - there were those who refused to accept that the more "ops" they flew, the longer were the odds against their survival. There were one or two such men on most of the squadrons, and their very presence could be good for morale: "If old Joe can live through two-and-half tours, I'm damn sure we can get through one!" It could also be bad, when the odds at last caught up with them: "If an ace like Joe can get the chop, what chance have we got?"

It was to one of the survivors - perhaps the most remarkable - that the major role in the attack on Mailly-le-Camp was entrusted: to Wing Commander Cheshire. He and his three picked Mosquito pilots from 617 Squadron, backed up by 83 and 97 Squadrons, late of PFF, would carry out the marking on the depot buildings. The way the 617 crews marked the target could be left to Cheshire; his selected method, with the bombing heights and timing, would be passed to the stations in time for squadron briefings. What the station staffs needed, as urgently as possible, was to know the chosen route, the bomb-load, the TOT - the time-on-target - and the bombing altitude. They needed this information in time for a thousand activities, on eighteen bomber airfields, to be undertaken, supervised and checked.

Leonard Cheshire

The 5 Group staff decided on the route. The Lancasters would fly from their bases, gaining height, via Reading, to leave the English coast at Beachy Head. By the time they reached the coast of France, just north of Dieppe, their height should be 12,000 feet. From there the route would run south-east for 200 miles, on a gradual descent, to reach the allotted bombing heights of between 6,000 and 8,000 feet at an assembly-point (or "datum-point") near the village of Germinon, nineteen miles north-north-west of the target. The wind at these altitudes was expected to be from 300 or 310 degrees at a speed of 30 to 35 miles per hour, and would be in the aircrafts' favour on their bombing runs.

If, for any reason, the attack were to be temporarily delayed, aircraft captains would carry out wide, left-hand orbits of the assembly-point, at heights between 8,000 and 12,000 feet, until called in to attack. Having bombed the target, they would maintain the same heading until they reached the next turning point ten miles further south, near the town of Troyes, where they would turn to starboard and fly westward past Fontainebleau, climbing on the way to regain 12,000 feet. At a point south of Paris, they would turn ten degrees north and fly for 160 miles to a pinpoint near Flers, and then due north to cross the coast at Arromanches. The cross-Channel leg would bring them to a landfall over Selsey Bill, and from there they would make their own way to their bases.

Each main force Lancaster would carry a bomb-load of one "cookie" - a 4,000-pounder - and either fifteen or sixteen 500-pounders, depending on the distance of their bases from the target, and, as the aim was to kill as well as to destroy, a proportion of the high explosive bombs would have the sort of casing that made a lot of flying fragments when the contents detonated. No incendiary bombs would be carried. From each aircraft, when the bombs began to fall, a 4.5 inch photo-flash would simultaneously drop out of the flare-chute, and the camera sequence would commence. The flash, fused to detonate at half the aircraft's altitude, would light the ground below - which should be the target area - with the equivalent of two hundred million candle-power. Three frames of film would pass through the camera, showing first the target, then the explosion of the bomb-load, and lastly its effect. The sequence lasted for exactly half a minute, and during that period a red light would glow on the instrument panel, warning the pilot to keep the aircraft straight and level. Not every pilot viewed those thirty seconds as the best part of the trip, but if he wanted to fly home with an aiming-point photograph - and everybody did - that was what he had to do. The fuel-load would be between 1,400 and 1,500 gallons of 100 octane petrol. Each aircraft would carry a hundred and eighty bundles of "window" (metal-foil strips to clutter up the enemy search radar-scopes), which the bomb-aimers would start dropping at the rate of one a minute as they approached the French coast, increasing to two a minute from the river Marne to a point beyond the target between Romilly and Sens, and continuing at the lower rate until they reached the Channel on the homeward route.

As to the TOT, there was a ready answer: whatever their army, and no matter how agreeable the local entertainment, soldiers off duty in the rearward areas were traditionally required to return to quarters before the clock struck twelve - in Service terminology, by twenty-three fifty-nine hours. H-hour for Cheshire's markers, therefore, would be 0001 hours - one minute after midnight - and the bombs would begin to fall on the depot five minutes later.

These basic elements of the tactical plan were signalled to the units, and the Group Headquarters staff, having lunched, directed their attention to the finer detail. So far, the plan must have seemed to be adequate. It is possible, with hindsight, to sense that deep within it lay the seeds of trouble - the enormous concentration on a very small target and the combination of one force with another unaccustomed to the method - but so far as the staff could tell, Mailly-le-Camp should be a nice, quiet trip.

CHAPTER TWO

THE SQUADRONS

It is a notable paradox that in the years between 1942 and 1945 the fertile fields of Lincolnshire, so peaceful through the centuries, provided the bases for what was until that time the most destructive, highly-trained fighting force in the history of warfare. F0rom 10,000 feet, on a clear night over Lincoln, you could see the Drem lighting systems of twenty bomber bases. They lay along the Heath, on the Wolds and coastal plain, and each had the capability of launching thirty-six Lancasters, every one of which could lift nearly ten tons of high explosive and incendiary bombs. On another six airfields - Heavy Conversion Units and Lancaster Finishing Schools - aircrews were trained to fly four-engined aeroplanes, to cope with emergencies, to work as a team on navigation exercises, to defend themselves in aerial combat and to drop their bombs with some degree of accuracy.

A standard Lancaster aircrew was composed of seven men: a pilot (who, in all normal circumstances, was captain of the aircraft), a navigator, a bomb-aimer (known in some squadrons as the air-bomber), a flight engineer, a wireless-operator, a mid-upper gunner and a rear gunner. Both the wireless-operator and the bomb-aimer were also qualified gunners, who could, when necessary, man one of the turrets. Many bomb-aimers, furthermore, had gained another task. All but a handful of the heavies were now equipped with H2S - the downward-looking radar whose emissions bounced back off the landscape to produce a crude black and white picture of such reflective features as coastlines, rivers and built-up areas. The apparatus had its limitations - it was useless over woodland, plains and open water - but its effectiveness was not constrained by range, as was that of Gee and Oboe; used with discrimination, in conjunction with other systems, it was an aid to navigation and, as a last resort, it could be used to aim the bombs. Who better, then, to use it than the man in the nose, whose gunnery and map-reading skills were seldom exercised on night operations, and whose main task lasted for only minutes on the bombing run? A quick, local course, and he had been re-graded as "bomb-aimer/set operator".

There were occasions when a Lancaster crew would be augmented by another man: new pilots would often accompany an experienced crew as "second dickies", certain pathfinder crews continued to include a "visual bomb-aimer" in addition to the set operator, and, in the aircraft of one squadron, as will be mentioned later, an extra man was carried for a special task.

A few bomber bases, dating from peacetime, boasted handsome buildings, well-established gardens and tree-lined avenues; the majority, of a later vintage, were less salubrious - Nissen huts and pre-fabs and miles and miles of mud. So far as their functions went, there was no great difference between these types of base. On the technical and flying sites of them all, bombs and pyrotechnics were stored, transported and hoisted into bomb-bays; thousands of rounds of .303 bullets were set in ammunition-trays and loaded into turrets; gun-sights were harmonised and bomb-sights levelled; petrol, oil and oxygen were piped into tanks and cylinders; parachutes, Mae Wests, dinghies and escape kits were scrupulously maintained; engines were overhauled, airframes patched and polished, and control-cables greased; hydraulic systems were bled and refurbished; compasses were swung and adjusted, radar sets and instruments were constantly serviced and re-calibrated.

On the 600-acre airfields, runways and taxi-tracks were swept, the systems of flare-path lights, glim-lamps, lead-in lights, Chance lights, goose-neck flares and beacons were checked; fire-engines and ambulances were always at the ready, and Bofors guns were manned. In Station offices and on domestic sites, adjutants wrote letters for the CO's signature to bereaved next-of-kin, dentists pulled teeth, doctors discouraged all forms of disability, chaplains led devotions and dispensed cocoa at de-briefings, clerks kept records, sentries did their duty, cooks did their worst, waitresses waited, batwomen batted, weather forecasters forecast, and orderlies fought their endless battles with disorder.

The aircrews on both sorts of airfield faced similar dangers in equivalent discomfort, the ground-crews spent the same long hours on distant, cold dispersals. But for the purposes of living, of sleeping, eating and passing off-duty hours, the amenities of the pre-war and the wartime bases were of a different order - as different as those of a luxury hotel and a sub-standard caravan-site. Strangely, morale was as high and results as respectable at one type of base as at another.

The 1 Group airfields lay to the north and east of Lincoln, between the city and the waters of the Humber estuary; the airfields of 5 Group, apart from Scampton and Dunholme Lodge, which were both north of Lincoln on either side of Ermine Street, lay south of Lincoln and eastward to the Fens.

Most bomber squadrons, at the stage the war had reached in 1944, had a "Unit Establishment" of twenty aircraft, but the strength might vary from one day to another, sometimes being more than the establishment and sometimes less, depending on losses and available replacements; furthermore, due to servicing requirements and the inevitable snags, the number of aircraft that could be actually deployed on any one night seldom equated with the strength. Each aircraft was identified by its squadron code-letters - "PH" for 12 Squadron, "KM" for 44 Squadron and so on - and by its own individual one-letter code - "A-Apple", for example, "B-Baker" or "C-Charlie". On the two-squadron airfields, of which there were several, the senior squadron's aircraft used up most of the alphabet, so the junior's aircraft had a number '2' painted on the fuselage alongside the letters, and their RT call-signs were "D-Dog Two", "E-Easy Two", et cetera.

1 Group's senior squadron, No. 12, with its fox's mask badge and motto

"Leads the Field", had a history dating from 1915. During the 1920s, the crews flew Fairey Foxes (hence the badge), with highly-polished cowlings which had brought the squadron its nickname of "The Shiny Twelve". In May 1940, based in France and equipped with Fairey Battles - obsolescent aircraft, and no match for the Messerschmitts - 12 Squadron had been tasked with the destruction of two metal bridges on the Albert Canal, across which Hitler's armies were marching into Belgium. The bridges were well-defended by guns and fighter aircraft, and, although the mission was clearly suicidal from the start, the five crews on stand-by volunteered to undertake it. Four were shot down, but several bombs had hit the bridges, and the first RAF Victoria Crosses of the war were posthumously awarded to Flying Officer Donald Garland (one of the section leaders), and to his observer, Sergeant Thomas Gray. Since then the squadron, having re-equipped with Wellingtons, had been based first at Finningley in Yorkshire, then at Binbrook and now, flying Lancasters, at the satellite airfield Wickenby, ten miles north-east of Lincoln on the road to Wragby.

100 Squadron, based at Waltham, near Grimsby, was the first British squadron to be specifically formed for a night-bombing role. It was the squadron's FE-2s which, in 1917, had destroyed the hangars of the Richthofen "Circus" at Douai. The squadron badge was a stark skull and crossbones, and the motto "Do not attack the hornet's nest" was rendered in Malay as "Sarang tebuan jangan dijolok", in recognition of early World War Two service in the Far East when, temporarily acting as a torpedo-bomber unit and flying antique Vickers Wildebeestes out of Singapore, the squadron had been engaged in a desperate attack upon the landing forces of the Japanese fleet.

Following Nos. 12 and 100 on the 1 Group Battle Order came 101 Squadron, based a few miles east of Market Rasen at Ludford Magna, known as Mudford Stagna to every airman and airwoman who had ever served there. Ludford tended to attract a number of visitors when mists lay over Lincolnshire, as it was one of the few bomber airfields to be equipped with FIDO, or "Fog, intensive dispersal operation" - a system of perforated pipes laid on each side of the main runway and filled with petrol which, when ignited, produced sufficient heat to burn off the lower layers of vapour. FIDO had first been used at Gravely in Huntingdonshire, when, in February 1943, Air Vice-Marshal Donald Bennett had tried it out himself; eventually, it had been installed at a dozen airfields, including the emergency landing grounds at Woodbridge and Carnaby, and the 5 Group base at Fiskerton. Ludford Magna was not, perhaps, the ideal site for the equipment, as a fog on the Wolds tended to arrive with an easterly breeze, which shifted the heated air a mile or two

downwind. Fido was thirsty - it thought nothing of consuming the equivalent
of fifty Lancasters' full fuel-loads in one hour's operation - and in action it
looked like the main street of Hell, but it did provide a haven for a pilot whose
base was clampers-dampers and who was not pyrophobic.

101 Squadron's badge showed a lion emerging from a battlement - a
device symbolising the power-driven turrets with which the squadron's aircraft
were the first to be equipped; the origin of the motto - "Mens agitat molem",
or "Mind over matter" - is less well-documented. In addition to their bomb-
loads, the squadron's Lancasters, since October 1943, had carried a radio-
jamming device code-named "Airborne Cigar", or "ABC", and an eighth crew
member - a German-speaking "special operator" - seated aft of the main spar
in the position where, in other aircraft, the rest-bed was located. Having tuned
his set to a radio frequency in use by a Luftwaffe controller, the special
operator would either drown out the messages with excruciating noises,
sometimes likened by non-Scotsmen to the sound of bagpipes, or would
broadcast bogus instructions to the listening fighter pilots. Whether, in due
course, the enemy's night-fighters found ways to home on these transmissions,
or whether the three big ABC aerials on the Lancasters' fuselage attracted
special attention, has never been clear, but the fact was that 101's casualty rate
tended to be higher than that of most main force squadrons.

Just off the A15 road south of the Humber, stood Elsham Wolds, the base
of 103 Squadron. Elsham was the most northerly of 1 Group's airfields, and
one of the three built to peace-time standards (the others were Binbrook and
the Lancaster Finishing School at Hemswell). From their RFC days of 1917,
No. 103 had always been a bomber squadron, equipped with the de Havilland
9 until 1919, and the Hawker Hind in the years between the wars. Authorised
by King George VI in 1937, 103's badge showed a black swan poised for
flight, and the motto offered the warning "Noli me tangere" - "Touch me not".
Having begun its World War II service flying Fairey Battles in France,
alongside 12 Squadron, No. 103 had progressed to Lancasters through
Wellingtons and Halifaxes and, since then, had played a full part in the
mounting night offensive.

No. 300 (Masovian) Squadron was based at Faldingworth, ten miles north
of Lincoln, where the river Ancholme begins its course to join the Humber.
One of four Polish bomber squadrons formed in 1940, No. 300 was the only
one still serving with the main force. Most of the early members had come
from Polish fighter units, and (as your author well remembers from the days
when he had the task of "converting" them to heavies) they continued to fly
with the kind of gay abandon more appropriate to the single-seat cockpit, the

oil-smeared goggles and the silk scarf fluttering in the breeze. On 8/9 October 1943, over Hannover, the Poles had dropped the last bombs to fall from Wellingtons in the course of World War 2; on 3/4 March 1944, they had flown the last-ever Wellington sortie - "gardening" off Lorient. Moving to Faldingworth, still with their Wellingtons, later in that month (they tended be rather more peripatetic than most), they had been the last 1 Group aircrews to re-equip with Lancasters.

Binbrook airfield, where Air Vice-Marshal Rice had formed the Special Duty Flight in April 1944, stood on the Wolds south-west of Grimsby. The base was blessed, as has been mentioned, with the buildings and facilities of pre-war days. When, in 1942, the airfield had been closed for a month or so while concrete runways were laid down for the new four-engined bombers, No. 12 Squadron, whose home it then was, had moved south to the unprepossessing satellite at Wickenby, with the promise of returning to Binbrook when the work was done. At that point, however, the staff of 1 Group Headquarters, with the sort of generosity only to be found in those who live and work in someone else's stately home, had handed Binbrook over to No. 460 Squadron of the Royal Australian Air Force. The crews of "Shiny Twelve", for their part, remained at Wickenby, and would do so for the duration of the war.

The complement of 460 Squadron was predominantly Australian, and the Station Commander, the gallant Group Captain Hughie Edwards, who had earned a VC over Bremen in 1941, was himself an Australian, albeit serving in the RAF. However, as the RAAF produced few flight engineers, and not many wireless operators, a number of British airmen found themselves "crewed up" at Binbrook, where they soon learned to say "G'die, dig" and to eschew saluting. Nor did all the Australian airmen in Britain serve on RAAF squadrons: most bomber squadrons had their Aussie complement, among whom were three courageous members of your author's crew; indeed, apart from Canada, Australia sent more of her sons to fight in the bomber war than any other country of the Empire and Commonwealth.

In the late autumn of 1943, Air Chief Marshal Harris had selected his objective for the winter. "We can wreck Berlin from end to end," he had told the Prime Minister, "if the USAAF will come in on it. It will cost four to five hundred aircraft. It will cost Germany the war". The older squadrons, reinforced by an influx of crews from the training schools and aircraft from the factories, had begun to spawn young ones to join them in the fray. "C" Flight of 12 Squadron, in which your author's crew was serving, had formed 626

Squadron at Wickenby almost overnight. (The new squadron, equally promptly and, in common with all the new squadrons, pending royal authority, had adopted the motto "To strive and not to yield", and a badge which appropriately depicted a seven-oared vessel on a stormy sea.) From its base at Elsham Wolds, No. 103 Squadron had provided Lancasters and crews to regenerate the ex-Wellington squadron, No. 166 (motto, "Tenacity"; badge, a ferocious-looking bulldog in full frontal aspect) at nearby Kirmington.

103 Squadron, with a little help from No. 101, had also produced No. 576 ("Carpe diem", or "Seize the opportunity", and a falcon bearing in its talons a Nazi-symbolising serpent), which shared Elsham Wolds with the parent squadron. 100 Squadron's "C" Flight, a prolific progenitor, had given birth to twins: 550 Squadron ("Per ignem vincimus" or "Through fire we conquer", and a fiery sword), which moved north-west up the Humber to North Killingholme, and 625 Squadron ("We avenge", and the rose of Lancaster in a seven-link chain) at Kelstern, between Louth and Market Rasen.

These were the squadrons of 1 Group which, with the Special Duty Flight at Binbrook, Air Vice-Marshal Rice would commit to the Mailly-le-Camp operation. Of the 5 Group squadrons, No. 9, the senior, was based at Bardney, beside the River Witham between Lincoln and Horncastle. The squadron badge, showing a bat in flight, complemented the motto "Per noctem volamus" or "We fly throughout the night". One of the squadron's first commanders, in its RFC days, had been a certain Major Hugh Dowding, later to be more widely known as C.-in-C. Fighter Command throughout the Battle of Britain. Six months after the Mailly-le-Camp operation, it was to be 9 Squadron's Lancasters, with those of No. 617, using the newly-acquired "SABS" (stabilised automatic bombsight) and 12,000 pound "Tallboy" bombs, which would overturn the Tirpitz as she lay in Tromsö Fiord. Then, on New Year's Day 1945, a 9 Squadron wireless operator, Flight Sergeant George Thompson, was to add a remarkable example of courage and selflessness to the bomber annals. When his aircraft was hit above the Dortmund-Ems Canal, a fire in the fuselage imperilled both the gunners, who were trapped in their turrets. Amid the exploding ammunition, despite being dreadfully burned himself, Thompson rescued them, one after another, beating out, with his bare hands, the flames which enveloped them. Thompson died of his injuries three weeks later and, although he never knew that his conduct had earned him the Victoria Cross, his colleagues knew well that they had served with a hero.

Next in seniority to No. 9 came 44 (Rhodesia) Squadron, based at Dunholme Lodge, four miles north of Lincoln. No. 44's motto was "Fulmina regis justa" - "The King's thunderbolts are righteous"; the badge, an African elephant, was based on the seal of a Matabele chief. Both the badge and the "Rhodesia" in the title recognised the contributions made by that colony, both in terms of aid to the war economy and of young men for the squadron. No. 44, too, had known an early commander, one Major A.T. Harris, who, in due course, was to attain higher rank and greater fame. At the beginning of 1942, Nos. 44 and 97 Squadrons (before the latter was transferred to the Pathfinder Force - indeed, before the PFF was formed), were the first to be equipped with the Avro Lancaster and, in that April, six crews from each squadron had made a spectacular attack on the Diesel engine plant at Augsburg in Bavaria - the first and last raid ever made by unescorted Lancasters in daylight at low-level. Of 44 Squadron's aircraft, four were shot down by Me-109s over France, and another was destroyed by gunfire over Augsburg, as were two of 97's. The Victoria Cross was awarded to the formation leader, Squadron Leader John Nettleton, a South African, whose aircraft, badly damaged, was the only one of 44 Squadron's to return.

The wartime-built airfield of Fiskerton, four miles east of Lincoln on the road to Wragby, was the base of 49 Squadron, another unit dating from 1916, and known since 1939, when the Air Ministry decided to promote civic interest in the RAF by affiliating certain squadrons to major towns and cities, as "Sheffield's Own". The squadron's record flying DH-4s in World War I had brought its aircrews ten DFCs, a Croix de Guerre and a DFM. The unit badge - a "greyhound courant" - was echoed in the motto "Cave canem", or "Beware of the dog". It was aircrews of No. 49 who, with 83 Squadron, had attacked the aqueduct above the Dortmund-Ems Canal, flying Handley-Page Hampdens, in August 1940 - a low-level night operation for which Flight Lieutenant "Babe" Learoyd was awarded the Victoria Cross.

Skellingthorpe airfield, in the woodland two miles west of Lincoln, was the home of No. 50 Squadron, whose motto was "Sic fidem servamus" - "Thus we keep faith". The squadron badge, which most observers took to represent a cloak and dagger, was in fact, and in heraldic terms, a mantle, severed by a sword, and marked a connection with Dover, where the squadron had been formed in 1916. In its Hampden days at Swinderby, further down the Fosse Way, No. 50 was commanded by the legendary "Gus" Walker, who had lost an arm when the bomb-bay contents of a crashed aircraft exploded while he was attempting to extricate the crew. "See if you can find the other glove," he had said, as they put him in the ambulance, "they're a new pair." The incident had ended Walker's playing days at Rugby (in due course he became a well-known referee), but had done nothing to limit his RAF career. Another squadron hero was Flying Officer Leslie Manser who, on the way back from Mannheim in

May 1942, had kept a badly damaged Avro Manchester in the air on one engine while his crew escaped by parachute. By the time they had jumped, it was too late for Manser, and his Victoria Cross was a posthumous award. Later, in 1943, 50 Squadron had released some of its best crews to form 617 Squadron; of these, Hopgood's and Maudslay's had died above the Möhne and Eder dams; the captain of another - the Australian Harold Martin - had become right-hand man to Guy Gibson and, in turn, to Leonard Cheshire. What "Micky" Martin didn't know about flying a Lancaster wasn't worth knowing, and many good judges rated him the best bomber pilot of them all.

57 Squadron was based at East Kirkby, ten miles inland from Skegness at the south end of the Wolds. Early in the war, the field had been a "K" site - a dummy aerodrome complete with flare-path, Whitley aircraft made of plywood and canvas, a fire-tender, an ambulance, searchlights and anti-aircraft guns - intended to draw the Luftwaffe's attention away from the genuine articles nearby. Then, in 1943, as the Command expanded, East Kirkby had ceased to be a decoy and become the real thing. 57 Squadron, whose aircrews had landed from their last operation at Scampton on 27 August, had moved in, set up shop and, three nights later, held a briefing by candle-light (the electrical contractors had not yet got around to the Operations Block) before sending fourteen Lancasters to attack Munschen Gladbach. The squadron motto, "Corpus non animum muto" ("My body changes, not my spirit"), and the phoenix badge, had been inspired by a few days in World War 1 when the entire aircrew strength, lost in action, had been replaced without a pause in operations.

No. 57 had sired its Berlin baby in November, when 630 Squadron arrived upon the scene. 630's motto, with a blunter theme than 57's, was "Nocturna Mori" and, during that winter, there had been a lot of "death by night". Indeed, the worst night in the history of Bomber Command had fallen on 30 March 1944, when eight hundred heavy bombers had been despatched to Nuremberg. The crews had experienced a combination of misfortunes - condensation trails signalling their passage through the skies of Germany, an unexpected wind-change which had thrown their timing out, and the night-fighter crews on the top of their form. Ninety-four aircraft had been lost over Europe, including four from East Kirkby, and another twelve had crashed on return. Five hundred and forty-five airmen had died in one night - more than all the RAF fighter pilots lost in the Battle of Britain.

A month before that terrible night, a 57 Squadron pilot, attempting his first operational take-off and developing a swing, had broken the undercarriage; as the aircraft slithered to a halt, the 4,000 pound cookie had detonated, and the blast had broken windows for many miles around.

Miraculously, the rear gunner, strapped inside his turret, had survived. A week or so later, two new pilots had reported for duty. Asked for their names, one had said "Monk", the other "Nunns". "That's all we need," the weary Flight Commander had commented, "a holy war."

Sharing Skellingthorpe with 50 Squadron was No. 61, whose motto was "Per purum tonantes" or "Thundering through the clear air". Originally formed in Essex as a fighter squadron in 1917, No. 61 had been regarded as "Hull's own" since the Air Ministry's public relations campaign of 1937. The squadron had nevertheless claimed the right to use the Lincoln Imp as its badge on being reformed at Hemswell as a bomber squadron. Its wartime crews had successively flown Hampdens, Manchesters and, since the Spring of 1942, Lancasters. On 3 November 1943, a squadron pilot, Flight Lieutenant William Reid, was badly wounded on the way to Düsseldorf; his windscreen was shattered, his controls damaged, and his intercom destroyed by a Bf-110. Telling no-one of his injuries, Reid had pressed on to the target. Next, a FW-190 had raked the bomber, killing the navigator, and wounding the flight engineer, the wireless operator fatally, and Reid himself again. The turrets and the oxygen system were put out of action. Still Reid had flown on to Düsseldorf - another two hundred miles - and bombed the centre of the target. Sometimes fainting from the loss of blood, half-frozen in the gale that was sweeping through the cabin, he had flown back to Skellingthorpe and made a safe landing. Reid's was the eleventh Bomber Command Victoria Cross of the war, and none was more deserved.

Nos. 83 and 97 Squadrons, transferred from 8 Group recently and reluctantly, if not to say acrimoniously, to provide 5 Group's "Illuminating Force", shared the peace-time base at Coningsby, five miles south-west of East Kirkby, near the castle of Tattershall, which served them as a landmark in that flat terrain just as the great cathedral served the squadrons based near Lincoln, and as the windmill at Old Bolingbroke served those at East Kirkby. No. 83's motto was "Strike to defend", its badge a red deer's antler with six points, which symbolised both the squadron's birthplace at Montrose in Scotland, and an epic night reconnaissance in 1918 when the two-man crews of the three aircraft committed each won the DFC. In August 1940, No. 83 had joined forces with 49 Squadron to attack the Dortmund-Ems canal and, a month later, a squadron wireless operator/air gunner, Sergeant John Hannah, had won the highest decoration: returning from a raid on the barges mustered at Antwerp for the invasion of Britain, he had put out a fire in the bomb-bay with his bare hands while rounds of ammunition exploded all around him, and helped his pilot to fly the Hampden home. It was 83 Squadron's present CO, Wing

Commander Laurence Deane, DFC, who was to be the Main Force Controller over Mailly-le-Camp.

97 (Straits Settlements) Squadron, formed at Waddington in 1917, had taken as its motto "Achieve your aim", and a downward-pointing arrow piercing a target as its badge. Since the historic Augsburg raid with 44 Squadron in April 1942, No. 97 had taken part in many major operations, including the thousand-bomber missions against Cologne, Essen and Bremen, the dusk attack on the Schneider works at Le Creusot and the first daylight raid on an Italian city. When No. 97 Squadron's aircrews had moved to Bourn in Cambridgeshire in April 1943 to join Don Bennett's Pathfinder Force, three crews had been left at Woodhall Spa to form the nucleus of a new 5 Group squadron - No. 619 - which now shared Dunholme Lodge with 44 Squadron. No. 619 had contrived to operate successfully, so far, with no apparent need of either badge or motto.

Metheringham airfield, ten miles south-east of Lincoln, was where "Newcastle's Own" 106 Squadron, after wartime lodgements in Rutland, Yorkshire and Nottinghamshire, had at last found a home. Like so many others, the squadron had progressed from Hampdens, through Manchesters, to the Lancasters with which it had been equipped since May 1942. It was only a week before the battle order for Mailly-le-Camp was posted in the briefing room that Sergeant Norman Jackson, one of the squadron flight engineers, had performed an act of extraordinary bravery: his aircraft had been hit after leaving Schweinfurt, and the starboard wing had begun to burn. Jackson, although wounded, had determined to deal with that fire. The fact that this had involved climbing out of an escape-hatch, carrying an extinguisher, and crawling along the wing in the teeth of a two hundred MPH air-flow, had not deterred him. Inevitably, he had been badly burned; inevitably, he had fallen. What remained of his parachute had saved his life. Jackson's VC had been the eighteenth awarded to an airman of Bomber Command.

Spilsby airfield, five miles west of Skegness, was the home of 207 Squadron which, in an previous incarnation, had been No. 7 Squadron of the Royal Naval Air Service in the first World War. With its winged lion badge, and its motto "Semper paratus", No. 207 had the dubious distinction of being the first squadron to operate the ill-fated, snag-infested Manchester, which its crews had flown with fortitude and difficulty from the start of 1940 until the end of 1942 when, having become inured to such jibes from other units as "207 Squadron's re-unions are always held in Stalagluft 3", they had been relieved to follow Nos. 44 and 97 in re-equipping with the Manchester Mark III - to be later and better known as the Lancaster Mark I.

Five miles south of Lincoln, on the road to Sleaford, stood Waddington, which had served the RFC as a training station in 1916, and had been a bomber base since 1937. Since the concrete runways were laid in 1943, it had predictably been occupied by two RAAF squadrons - Nos. 463 ("Press on regardless", and four sledge-hammers on a seven-pointed star) and 467, whose motto and badge were too irreverent to be awarded official recognition. Irrationally, in an arithmetic sense, 467 had been the first to form - at Scampton, towards the end of 1942 - and had taken a full part in the main force campaign. Perhaps the squadron's worst period had come after the move to Waddington when, in August 1943, it had lost the Squadron Commander on one night, his replacement three nights later and a further three crews - two of whom were flying their first operations - in the great Hamburg fire raids. On 25 November, 467 had spawned 463 who, with the precocity expected of Australians, had achieved sufficient adult status within twenty-four hours to join in the Battle of Berlin.

617 Squadron had been formed at Scampton, in the spring of 1943, for the specific purpose of breaking the Ruhr dams, and that famous action was depicted in its badge and remembered in the motto "Après moi, le deluge", or "After me, the flood". Since then, the squadron had moved south-east to Woodhall Spa, which had been No. 97's base for the attack on the Diesel plant at Augsburg in 1942. The amenities at Woodhall had seemed meagre after Scampton's, and the officers had promptly commandeered the Petwood Hotel in the village to serve them as a Mess. Although officially a main force squadron, No. 617 had maintained its status as a special force, not to be employed on the nightly grind to distant German cities, but on such specific targets as factories, railway yards and viaducts. The dams raid had been daring and hazardous, but so had many others: it was the skill in the use of new, exciting methods and equipment - the Barnes Wallis bouncing bomb, the synchronised spot-lights for judging height above the water, and the low-level bombsight which had made the Dam Busters' reputation - that and the skill and spirit of their Squadron and Flight Commanders. Squadron Leader Dave Shannon DSO DFC, of the RAAF, was one of these. As a Flight Lieutenant, the Australian had been flying with No. 106 at Syerston, when Guy Gibson, his CO, had been posted to Scampton under orders from Cochrane to form the new squadron. Gibson had carte blanche to pick his own crews, and Shannon had quickly found himself with 617. As last man in the third "Vic" to attack the Möhne dam, he was on his bombing run when the structure cracked and the waters of the Möhne had broken through. Gibson, telling Shannon to save his bouncing bomb, had led the squadron on to attack the Eder dam, where

Shannon had made six runs, none of which had satisfied him. Henry Maudslay had tried, also unsuccessfully, and was never seen again. Shannon had at last launched his bomb - and missed. It had been left to Les Knight, another Australian, to break the Eder dam.

It was for his determination and persistence that Shannon had received his DSO, and the investiture had coincided with his 21st birthday. Well-briefed, King George VI had advised a celebration and, late that night, Shannon had attributed his condition to the Royal Command. At that time, Shannon, golden-haired and slender, had the appearance of a boy. Embarrassed by this, he had grown a large moustache to camouflage his looks and, simultaneously, fallen in love with a WAAF Intelligence Officer. The moustache and Ann Fowler, however, had proved incompatible, and he had sacrificed the one to wed the other. In September 1943, still with 617 Squadron, he had been sent to attack the Dortmund-Ems Canal (a highly dangerous and perennial assignment). Finding it at last, after searching for an hour or so, he had failed to hit the aiming point. He had been more successful with the Gnome-Rhone engine factory at Limoges, marked at low level by Cheshire and Martin, and had dropped a 12,000 pounder on the centre of the plant. After nine more such bombs from the other squadron Lancasters, the engine plant had disappeared. Then, when Leonard Cheshire got his Mosquitos, Shannon, with Flight Lieutenant Dave Kearns, a New Zealander, and Flight Lieutenant Gerry Fawke, had been chosen to fly them.

627 Squadron, with Mark BIV Mosquitos, on its detachment from 8 Group in April, had joined No. 617 at Woodhall Spa. The squadron had first formed at Oakington in Cambridgeshire in the previous November, and had adopted the motto "At first sight" and, as a badge, a striking representation of a diving hawk with a firebrand in its beak. No. 627's tasks since then, apart from target-marking, had included bombing operations, "Windowing", photographic reconnaissance and even an occasional "Gardening" trip. It was to be with 627 that Wing Commander Guy Gibson's life, and his long, brave career as a bomber pilot, would end: he crashed in Holland on 20 September 1944, returning from an attack on Rheydt in the Ruhr for which he had volunteered to act as Master Bomber. Perhaps the squadron crews' most memorable mission, and the most satisfying, was to come eight months after the Mailly-le-Camp raid when, on New Year's Eve 1945, they would attack and destroy the Oslo Headquarters of the German Gestapo.

A number of the "Berlin baby" squadron crews were still on strength when the time came around for Mailly-le-Camp - not a large number, for the campaign had taken heavy toll. The C.-in-C.'s forecast had been correct in that regard: the Battle of Berlin had cost five hundred aircraft, and more than another nine hundred had been damaged. It had not, however, cost Germany the war. But then, the C.-in-C. had prefaced his promise with the proviso "If the USAAF will come in on it". They had not: they had stuck to their doctrine of precision bombing, against such strategic targets as they considered feasible and, what was more, in following that policy, they had brought the Luftwaffe to combat with such effect that the General of Fighters, Adolf Galland, had painted a dark picture for his masters in Berlin. "Between January and March 1944," he told them, "our day-fighter arm lost more than a thousand pilots. They included our best Staffel, Gruppe and Geschwader commanders. The time has come when our force is in sight of collapse".

Notwithstanding this cri de coeur, the fact was that the Generalmaior still had at his command over seven hundred day-fighters, mostly single-engined Bf-109s and FW-190s, and - perhaps more significantly in the context of this story - nearly five hundred radio-controlled, radar-guided night-fighters, Bf-110s, Ju-88s and Do-217s, reinforced by freelancing day-fighters who hunted down their prey by the light of flares and searchlights, and who could find them that much quicker by the light of the moon.

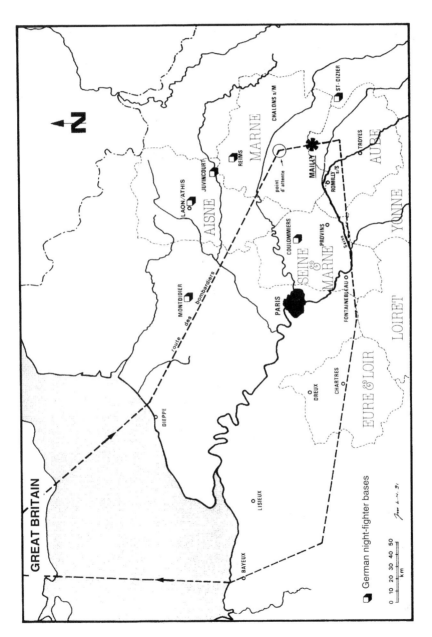

Attack Route for Mailly-le-Camp, 3/4 May, 1944.

CHAPTER THREE

THE PLAN

By midday on Wednesday 3rd May, the name of one French village, however mispronounced, had gained a currency in England that it had not had before. On the airfields of Nos.1 and 5 Group, those who had the need to know - the Commanding Officers, their immediate subordinates and operations staffs, plus, so it was rumoured, the barmaids at most of the licensed premises in Lincolnshire - were aware that close beside that village lay the target for tonight. The appropriate section leaders knew by what route and at what time the bombers had to get there, and the bomb-loads they would carry. The remainder of the plan - the height to bomb, the way the target would be marked, who would be in charge and how he would communicate - had yet to be revealed.

As to the bombing altitude, although remarkable advances in the technique of high-level bombing had been achieved since the early days of the war, the fact remained that the longer a bomb was in the air, the more its trajectory was affected by imperfections in its shape and changes in the wind velocity, and the less its chances were of falling on the target. Ideally, bombs would be dropped from the lowest altitude compatible with safety; high enough, that is, for the aeroplane itself to be above the range of blast and flying fragments from the detonations, and the accepted rule of thumb was a thousand feet of altitude for every thousand pounds of high explosive in the biggest bomb. In the real world, however, the reaction of the enemy had to be considered, and the reason why the heavies normally bombed from the greatest altitude they could reasonably attain was that the same disruptive forces of wind and of friction also affected the trajectory of anti-aircraft shells. The so-called light flak could be effective up to nine or ten thousand feet; the heavy flak reached to over twenty thousand - above the ceiling of a loaded Halifax or Stirling, and close to that of the higher-flying Lancasters. For Mailly-le-Camp, where the defences were expected to be light, it had been decided, as a compromise between the requirements of prudence and of accuracy, that the bombing heights would range from 6,000 to 8,000 feet, and individual thousand-foot slots were allocated to the squadrons within those chosen altitudes.

Among the other details, elements of mystery remain. Indeed, the fact has to be faced that to discover what went wrong in the half-hour after midnight on 3/4 May is to tackle an enigma which has puzzled students of the bomber war for over forty years. The documents, the Service forms and records, are often mutually contradictory, and the memory of the surviving participants cannot be expected, at this distance, to be photographic. The best that can be done - at least, the best that your author can do - is to follow the procedure he was taught at the RAF Intelligence School in the nineteen-fifties: collect, collate and evaluate the information; in other words, sift through the evidence and pick the most convincing. In the matter of the marking, this presents no problem, because it comes from one who, at that same establishment in Parliament Square, would have been regarded as an A1 source - "A" for authenticity and "1" for credibility.

It was Leonard Cheshire's habit, so soon as he awoke, to write a report for Group Headquarters on the previous night's operation while the facts were still clear in his mind. This was what he wrote in the early afternoon of Thursday, 4th May:

"On return from leave, the Squadron was called upon to carry out the initial marking of the military barracks at Mailly-le-Camp for 300 Lancasters of the Main Force. Permission was not granted for the rest of the Squadron to take any part in the attack. The plan, which was hurriedly made because orders were not received until late in the day, was designed to achieve tactical surprise and speed. Intelligence sources reported that the barracks housed upwards of a front line armoured division, and consequently it was hoped to start the bombing before any troops could escape out of the area. The attack was scheduled to start at midnight, one minute after all good soldiers have booked in at the guard-room. In order to deal with the large force of aircraft employed, the bombing was to be carried out in two waves, the first at zero hour on a marker dropped in the eastern of the three main barrack blocks, and the second eighteen minutes later on a marker in the western block..."

Of the two waves of bombers, it had been agreed between the two Air Vice-Marshals that No. 5 Group would provide the first and No. 1 the second. The other part of the agreement - that a small force of 1 Group aircraft, led by Rice's SD Flight, were to attack a "special target" within the depot area - appears to have been unknown to Leonard Cheshire; at least, if he were told of it, he did not recall it later.

It was at this point that the plan departed from the format which had so far served the bombers well. For over six months, the big Command attacks had been directed over air-to-air voice radio - RT, that is - by a Master Bomber, sometimes known by the crews as the Master of Ceremonies, or "MC". The method had originally been employed by Wing Commander Guy Gibson in 617 Squadron's attack on the Ruhr dams in May 1943; it had been developed by 5 Group in the following month on the Friedrichshafen raid, and adopted by 8 Group for the full-scale operation against the V-Weapon establishment at Peenemunde on 17/18th August 1943, when Wing Commander "Honest John" Searby of 83 Squadron won the DSO for his work as Master Bomber (there are those who will remember the sound of his voice in their headphones, clear and confident, as they came in from the Baltic on the run-up to the target: "Aim for the centre of the green TIs").

Since then, the 8 Group techniques had been developed further; the methods of marking and of aiming bombs had been refined. Now, the marking could be "off-set" from a smoke-obscured objective, and the bomb-sights programmed with a carefully-calculated false wind, which would result - or should result - in bombs on the target; there were highly-skilled "Primary Markers" and relays of "Backers-up" to maintain an accurate aiming-point throughout the attack. But the task of the Master Bomber, usually of

Squadron Leader or Wing Commander rank and always an experienced campaigner, hadn't greatly changed. It was still his task to concentrate the bombing, to discourage "creep-back" (the tendency to let the bombs go early and get the hell out of there), and to provide a voice of recognisable authority in a cold and hostile sky. He was the first to arrive at the target, and usually the last to leave; his life, and the lives of his crew, were in jeopardy throughout; in large measure, the results of the attack depended on his judgement. If Command HQ could relate operations to a risk-factor, as they recently had with those to France, there was a good case for every Master Bomber mission to count double.

As with the techniques, the thinking had developed: the 8 Group Master Bomber method had been fine for the targets of 1943, when most of the high explosive and incendiaries dropped (131,464 out of 157,457 tons) were on the main centres of industry and administration (the fact that it had also been fine for the Peenemunde rocket establishment - a target also attacked in moonlight at comparatively low level, and not totally dissimilar to the tank depot - seems to have been disregarded), but now Ralph Cochrane had the bomber chief's ear. Mailly-le-Camp was a 5 Group operation, and would be run the 5 Group way. There would be no Master Bomber as such; his functions would be divided between a "Marker Leader" and a "Main Force Controller" or, failing him, his designated deputy. Cheshire, as Marker Leader, would initiate, supervise and organise the low-level marking. When he was satisfied about the first set of markers, he would inform the Controller who, if equally content, would call the bombers in. As the attack developed, Cheshire would order such backing-up by the ex-PFF Lancasters of 83 and 97 Squadrons on the initial markers as seemed to be required. The same sequence would be followed for the second aiming-point. With these arrangements, another little seed of disaster was dropped into the fertile soil of the operational plan. There were more to come.

It is true to say of communications, especially in warfare, that the simpler the system, the more chance there is of the message getting through, and although the system devised for Mailly-le-Camp seemed reasonably straightforward, it had an elementary flaw: few of the participants knew anything about it. This appears to have been due to a mistaken impression, somewhere along the line, that the aircraft of 1 Group were using different frequencies from those of 5 Group. The explanation of this may lie in the fact that the enterprising Cochrane, in his best baronial style, had recently arranged for his Lancasters to be equipped with VHF (in the 30 to 300 megahertz range), hitherto only available to fighters, which gave better voice reception than the

HF channels (3 to 30 megahertz) used by other bomber groups; what seems to have been overlooked within the 5 Group plan was that Baron Rice of Bawtry had promptly done the same. In view of the supposed discrepancy, it was apparently decided, either at Grantham or at Coningsby, that the Main Force Controller's orders would be passed to the Lancasters by his wireless operator, using Morse code transmissions on WT - a facility shared by all - all, that is, except for the Mosquitos, which carried neither wireless operators nor WT.

Taking H-hour as the time at which the target would be marked, the plan required three PFF Mosquitos, using "Oboe", to illuminate the depot with green cascading target-indicators (TIs) at H-hour minus three minutes. Cheshire had the next three minutes in which to ensure that the TIs were falling on the right piece of France and, by their light, to identify the initial, eastern aiming-point. He and his deputy, Squadron Leader Shannon, would then drop slow-burning 250-pound incendiaries, known in the business as spot fires, as markers for the bomb-aimers in the 5 Group Lancasters. A further six minutes were allowed for Cheshire to check these markers, which would be coloured red, in conjunction with the Main Force Controller, and either to improve on them or to tell the Controller to call the first wave in. (Some surviving airmen recall that the broadcast message for 5 Group would be "Rat One, bomb", and that the 1 Group aircraft would be called on as "Rat Two"). If any delay occurred, either in the marking or the consultation with the Controller, the main force pilots were to occupy themselves in making left-hand orbits at pre-determined heights around the assembly-point, marked for their convenience by a succession of yellow TIs.

The time would now be approaching H plus five, and during the next six minutes a hundred and seventy-three Lancasters of 5 Group would fly across the target at heights between six and eight thousand feet, on a southerly heading, and unload their cargoes on the red spot fires, or as close to them as the limitations of their bomb-sights and their weapons would allow.

Meanwhile, and all unknown to the Marker Leader and the Main Force Controller, four Lancasters of 1 Group's SD Flight would mark the "special target" with green spot fires, and thirty Lancasters of the 1 Group main force would be directed to attack. This part of the action, according to the operational order from Bawtry, would be controlled by a "1 Group MC", but only those immediately involved seem to have been aware of that.

By H plus eleven, the simultaneous attacks on the "special target" and the easterly aiming-point would be complete, and Cheshire's second pair of Mosquitos would have the next nine minutes in which to mark the westerly aiming-point with another set of red spot fires for the main body of the 1

Group force - a hundred and forty Lancasters - which would by then have arrived at the assembly-point to meet a scheduled TOT of between H plus twenty minutes and H plus twenty-six (0021 to 0027 hours). To ensure that the low-flying Mosquito crews were not discomforted by a hail of heavy objects falling on them from above, bombing would cease for those nine minutes, and would not recommence until Cheshire had approved the new markers. If it were necessary, the broadcast order from the Controller would be "Rat Two, wait", at which the 1 Group Lancasters would orbit the assembly-point at their allotted heights. When the western markers had been passed as satisfactory, the Controller would transmit "Rat Two, bomb", and the final phase of the attack would begin.

Elements of three night-fighter wings, or Nachtjagdgeschwadern (NJG), were based within range of the bomber's outbound route. NJG 1 deployed No. III Gruppe (roughly the equivalent of an RAF squadron), with eleven Messerschmitt Bf-110s, at Athies-sur-Laon, fifty miles to the north; NJG 4's No. I Gruppe, with twenty Bf-110s and Ju-88s, was just across the Belgian border at Florennes, No. II Gruppe was at Coulommiers, twenty-five miles east of Paris, with fifteen Bf-110s and Dornier 217s, and No. III Gruppe was at Athies with a similar mixture of sixteen aircraft; also at Athies was No. III Gruppe of NJG 5 with another twenty aircraft; forty-five miles east of Mailly-le-Camp, at St. Dizier, were ten Bf-110s and Me-410s of I Gruppe NJG 5. Of these ninety-two night-fighters, approximately sixty could be expected to be serviceable at any one time.

Also at hand were three day-fighter wings - Jagdgeschwadern 3, 5 and 27 - with some hundred and fifty single-engined Messerschmitt Bf-109s and Focke-Wulf 190s between them. A number of these "Wilde Saue" might come to the assistance of their night-fighter comrades - the "Zahme Saue" - but the main threat to the bombers would always be from the radio-directed and radar-equipped Bf-110s and Ju-88s.

The Bf-110G ("Gustav" to the pilots), with a wing-span of just over 53 feet, a length of 40 feet, four inches and a maximum weight of 22,000 pounds, was not, in its dimensions, unlike the Mosquito, although, with its square-tipped wings and twin fins and rudders, it was not so sleek in appearance; powered by two 1,150 horse-power Daimler-Benz engines and crewed by a pilot, a wireless-operator and a flight mechanic/gunner, it had a ceiling of 26,250 feet, a range of 1,300 miles and a top airspeed of 342 mph (some 40 mph slower than the Mosquito); it was armed with four cannons in the nose - two 30 mm and two 20 mm - and twin rear-mounted 7.9 mm machine-guns.

The Junkers 88C was the night-fighter version of an aircraft which the Luftwaffe had used as a medium bomber since the first days of the war. It had the single tall tail-fin characteristic of the makers and, with a wing-span of nearly 64 feet, a length of over 47 feet and a maximum weight of 28,900 pounds, it was a considerably bigger aircraft than the Bf-110. Normally, it had a crew of two, and the twin 1,200 horse-power Junkers Jumo engines gave it a ceiling of 30,000 feet, a 1,230 mile range and a maximum airspeed of 307 mph; its armament comprised three 20 mm cannon and three 7.9 mm machine-guns in the nose, with a 13 mm machine-gun in the rear of the cockpit.

In the ever-escalating electronic war the opposing scientists constantly vied with each other to produce a better search-radar, a more cunning counter-measure or a more effective jammer, and the night-fighters' air-to-air equipment had been recently up-dated. The "Himmelbett" ground-to-air control system, based on a chain of "Giant Würzburg" radars, could no longer be relied on: the "Himmelbett" ("bed with a canopy") ground stations were limited in the number of contacts they could handle at any one time and were liable to be swamped by a major attack. Furthermore, Bomber Command's introduction of "Window" in the late summer of 1943 had reduced the canopy to shreds. It had become an urgent requirement to produce radars with a longer range and a better performance than the "Lichtenstein" sets in the night-fighters' cockpits.

Emil Nonnenmacher was one of the pilots who used the new equipment: "In the beginning of April," he told your author, "we were temporarily posted to an airfield near Berlin to do some special training with a new 'wonder weapon'. It was top secret at that time, of course. We were convinced it would give us superiority in the air - for a while, anyway. Until then, it had been hard enough to find a bomber, let alone knock it down. Now, this was not a problem any more. The apparatus, called officially FuG227, code-name 'Flensburg', transmitted a strong signal in a narrow beam which came back, like echoes, from the bomber's 'Monica' tail warning device. By following these signals and putting on speed to catch up with the target - well, it made night-fighting the easiest thing in the world. The main advantage was the range - more than 100 kilometres, compared with not much more than 7 for the 'Lichtenstein'."

Other air-to-air radars coming into service were "SN-2", which, although it had the advantage of operating outside the frequency jammed by "Window", had a restricted range, and "Naxos-Z", which produced the same sort of echo from the bomber's H2S as 'Flensburg' did from the 'Monica' transmissions.

In addition to their normal armament, many night-fighters had two upward-firing 20 mm cannons, mounted either in the fuselage, in the Ju-88s, or at the back of the cabin in the Bf-110s. These guns, known in the Luftwaffe as "Schräge Musik" ("slanting music" or "Jazz"), were aimed by the pilot by means of a reflector-sight and, firing upward at an angle of seventy or eighty degrees, gave him the deadly capability of attacking the bomber from its blind spot - underneath the fuselage. Although "Schräge Musik" had entered the NJGs' armoury in the late summer of 1943 and, since then, had been the cause of many deaths among the bomber crews, the RAF Intelligence Branch had only recently become aware of its existence, perhaps because, as its ammunition included no tracer, not even the survivors ever knew what hit them.

From nicknames dating back to World War I, the German pilot was an "Emil" and his observer was a "Franz", a friendly appellation which had introduced a new word to the Luftwaffe vocabulary: to "franzen" was to find your way from 'A' to 'B'. When the requirement came, in the Ju-88, for someone to act as pilot's mate - to handle the fuel cocks, pump the de-icer, control the heating and activate the weapons - he was selected from the ground-crew and known as "the mixer".

In a Luftwaffe night-fighter's cockpit the need for a rapport between the pilot and his crew was essentially the same as it was in the cabin of an RAF bomber, and it often included the same semi-serious element of rivalry. "I'm the captain of the aircraft", the pilot might remark, "and I make the decisions." "Come off it," the navigator would respond, "you're just a driver. You wouldn't know which way to turn if I didn't tell you." Such internal sniping was as common and as natural in a Bf-110 or a Ju-88 as it was in a Lancaster or a Mosquito, nor was it all the opposing airmen had in common. They spent the same dark hours in the sky over Europe, they were similarly dependent on the skill of their crew-mates, and equally reliant on their equipment and machinery; each flew with the intention of destroying his enemy and the knowledge that his enemy might destroy him; none wanted to be killed, but realised that he could be and, furthermore, that tonight might be the night.

The most successful crews, whether bomber or night-fighter, shared certain attributes. They were skilful and steadfast; they knew when to exercise a modicum of caution, and when to throw it to the winds; they were constantly alert and worked well together as a team. In none of these ways were they superior to the average good crew. The difference was that they enjoyed a lot of luck. Given luck, and all the other factors, survival was possible, even fame and favour.

Fame, in fact, among night-fighter pilots, whether of the Luftwaffe or the RAF, was for the very few. There were many who flew nightly and seldom fired a shot in anger, and some who were successful every now and then; the elite - the "experten" - were those who, blessed with both the skill and the fortune to claim a few successes early in their flying careers, tended to continue in that vein: thereafter they had the first place on the battle order, were nearest to the runway on the readiness apron, and got the controller's first word of guidance when he had a radar contact. Every Nachtjagdgeschwader had two or three such aces, all of whom could count their "shoot-downs" in high numbers. It was there, for the bomber crews, that Lady Luck came in. They might fly throughout a tour and never meet a fighter, or only meet the "Emils" who were not the best of shots. But, if their luck was out, they were likely to tangle, sooner or later, with one of the triers who was having a good night or, worst of all, with one of the "experten". The tactical arrangements for Mailly-le-Camp made it almost certain that a number of bomber crews would do exactly that.

That a planning staff could contemplate, or a commander countenance, any plan of action in which a possibility existed - even a remote one - of several hundred fully-laden Lancasters orbiting a marker, in bright moonlight, within striking range of at least four night-fighter bases, staggers the imagination. Luftwaffe Headquarters, given the chance, could not have planned it better. If the seeds of havoc had already been sown in the groundwork of the plan, here were the rain and the sunshine to ensure their germination.

That criticism, however, is formed with the advantage of hindsight; it is clear that, at the time, no-one saw reason to expect disaster. Indeed, by the standards of Bomber Command, it may have seemed unlikely that the night of Wednesday, 3rd May 1944 would be a night to remember - not one to be recorded in the annals of the air war as particularly spectacular, like the thousand-bomber raids on Essen and Cologne, the breaking of the dams, or the attacks on the Diesel plant in Augsburg and the rocket base at Peenemunde, nor as peculiarly dire as the Battle of Berlin or the Nuremberg raid of the 30th March. Less than half the bomber strength would be engaged, and none of the planned operations was of a sort to provide Thursday morning's papers with more than a column or two of straightforward copy from the Air Ministry hand-out.

While Nos. 1 and 5 Groups were attending to the tank depot at Mailly-le-Camp, Air Vice-Marshal Bennett would be sending his six remaining heavy squadrons, with a small Mosquito marker force, to attack the Luftwaffe aircraft stores and equipment depot at Montdidier, which lay south-east of Amiens in the valley of the Somme, a few miles to the north of, and a third of the way along, the outbound course to Mailly-le-Camp. The H-hour for Montdidier would be twenty minutes after midnight, by which time the main attack should be in its final phase. A lone Mosquito crew of No. 1409 Met. Flight at Wyton would carry out the usual pre-attack weather reconnaissance above the target areas and radio their findings to both attack leaders. Meanwhile, some thirty Mosquitos of 8 Group's Light Night Striking Force, as a change from their nightly "nuisance" raids on Berlin, would bomb a chemical works in the Rhineland town of Ludwigshaven, and another twelve Mosquitos would attack an ammunition dump at Châteaudun, to the west of Orleans, and south of the main force's homeward course from Mailly-le-Camp.

The public houses, cinemas and dance-halls of the North and East Ridings could expect to do good business on Wednesday evening, for the activities of Nos. 4 and 6 Groups would be confined to the despatch of thirty Yorkshire-based Halifaxes on "Gardening" (the code-name for mine-laying operations in European waters), from St. Nazaire in the south to the Frisian Islands in the north.

No. 100 Group would put three RCM Halifaxes in the air over France to interfere with the enemy radio and radio early-warning systems, and thirteen of the Group's "Bomber Support and Intruder" Mosquitos would do their best to make life unpleasant for the Nachtjagdgeschwader crews.

The three OTU Groups, Nos. 91, 92 and 93, would allow thirty-four of their more advanced trainee crews to venture out on "Nickels" - scattering morale-boosting leaflets from their Wellingtons and Whitleys over sleeping towns and villages in northern France.

From their bases in East Anglia, an assortment of No. 3 Group aircraft - Halifaxes, Stirlings and Lysanders - would fly on "special operations", a term which covered the delivery of SOE agents and clandestine supply drops to the French Resistance.

In support of the main heavy bomber operations, the ADGB (Air Defence of Great Britain, as Fighter Command, for some arcane reason, had been re-named at the end of 1943), planned to send fifteen Mosquito light-bombers of No. 2 Group to attack night-fighter airfields, and eight fighter Mosquitos to patrol the target areas.

The strategic attack on Montdidier apart, these were routine operations of a sort that were mounted night after night. The main event was Mailly-le-Camp, and it is time, in this account, to consider the complement of that establishment. It was a mixed bag of battle-tanks, self-propelled guns and armoured vehicles which the Wehrmacht had assembled at the old French Army depot. "Klotzen, nicht Klecken", or "strike with the fist, don't tickle with the fingers" - that was the advice which General Heinz Guderian, the pioneer and chief protagonist of German tank warfare, had given his panzer divisions in the all-conquering days of 1940 and 1941, when they and the Stuka squadrons - which together had been the embodiment of Blitzkrieg - had romped through Western Europe, Poland and the Balkans. Since those years, however, the pace of war had changed, and the war-winning potential of the Wehrmacht's main striking force had steadily declined. Battles were no longer won by rapid manoeuvre, but by slow, remorseless attrition; not by spectacular actions in the field, but by the steady deployment of overwhelming manpower and technical resources.

The years had taken toll of the units now marshalled at the depot. A panzer division of the early days would have comprised a tank brigade of two four-battalion regiments, with a strength of some 560 tanks between them, two panzer-grenadier (infantry) regiments with trucks and motor-cycles, an artillery regiment, an anti-tank battalion, a reconnaissance battalion, an engineer battalion and a communications unit. By the summer of 1943, the panzer divisions (with the exception of Hitler's pride and joy, the Waffen SS Division) were down to one tank battalion, usually of three companies with seventeen tanks each. And whereas, in the past, there would have been a judicious mixture of light and medium tanks, there was now no option: they had to be content with what there was.

Together with the 15th Division, the 21st Division had formed Generalfeldmarschall Rommel's Afrika Korps in 1942. Although opposed by four times their number, they had swept across the North African desert, almost to Alexandria, before shortages of fuel and ammunition had brought them to a halt. The 21st Division had been badly mauled at Alam Halfa and suffered further losses at El Alamein. The Afrika Korps, with scant support from Berlin, outnumbered six-to-one and under constant air attack, had been reduced to eleven German and ten Italian tanks. The 21st, as a fighting force, had been totally destroyed - tanks, anti-tank guns, sappers and panzer-grenadiers. It had been reformed in Normandy in July 1943 and, in its present role as a training formation, comprised a one-battalion regiment of obsolescent tanks, captured from the French in the early days of 1940, two grenadier regiments, a small artillery component and a recce unit.

Among the armour withdrawn from the eastern front, and now temporarily based at Mailly-le-Camp, was the Panzerkampfwagen IV, 23.6 tons in weight, with a long-barrelled, armour-piercing 76 mm gun. In many experts' opinion, the Panzer IV was the most important German tank of World War 2 - both in terms of numbers and of tactical achievement. Its lighter predecessor, the Czech-built twenty-ton Panzer III, armed with a 50 mm gun, had been highly successful in the campaigns of the early 1940s but, when

Hitler launched Operation Barbarossa in 1941, it had proved no match for the Red Army's Diesel-engined T-34. Even the Panzer IV, its replacement, could not equal the fire-power of the Russian tanks, and it was not until M.A.N. of Augsburg designed the forty-six ton Mark V Panther, powered by a V-12 Maybach engine with double the horse-power of the earlier marks, that the Wehrmacht found a battle-tank that could hold its own, not only against those of the Red Army, but against any in the world.

Panther tank on a wagon at Mailly-le-Camp.

Also based at Mailly-le-Camp were a few Tiger tanks, heavily-armoured, fifty-six tons in weight, powered by even more powerful Maybach V-12 engines. The Tiger was manned by a crew of five: the commander, a gunner and a loader in the turret, with the driver and a wireless operator/gunner in the hull. The Tiger's armament consisted of a long-barrelled 88 mm Kwk 36 gun and a 7.92 mm machine-gun in the turret, another 7.92 mm gun in the front armour-plate and a 9 mm machine-carbine stowed in the hull. It was equipped with six smoke-generators and three mine-throwers, and it carried five thousand rounds for the machine-guns, ninety-two rounds of ammunition for the 88 mm, and a hundred and twenty-five gallons of fuel for the Maybach engine. It had a serviceable radio, an excellent binocular telescope and could make its way through water to a depth of fifteen feet. With all these advantages, however, the Tiger's bulk made it hard to manoeuvre, and the Panzertruppen nicknamed it the "Furniture Van". The 700 bhp Maybach, as it happened, was not particularly reliable and, when it broke down, recovery of the monster was frequently impossible. The Tiger, nevertheless, was an effective mobile fortress, and those who had been in a position to judge have stated that the sight of it, advancing at a steady 25 mph with all guns blazing, was conducive to a state of muscular paralysis. It was to be a single Tiger, in the hedgerows of Normandy one month later, which would destroy twenty-five Allied tanks and vehicles before retiring unscathed, having blocked the advance of the entire 7th Armoured Division. That Tiger was commanded, however, by an exceptional Panzer man, Leutnant Michael Wittmann (who, for his action, was awarded the Knight's Cross); the fact was that the Tiger tanks, and their subsequent developments, although good value in a defensive battle, were a very far cry from the fast-moving strike force of Guderian's dream.

The morale of the Panzertruppen gathered at the depot, the tank-crews, the gunners and the panzer-grenadiers, may not have been so high as it had been in their all-conquering days of the European Blitzkrieg. Nevertheless, they wore on their tunics the Panzer battle badge (a tank with a swastika poised above the driver's hatch, crowned by an eagle and surrounded by a laurel wreath), and although their fighting vehicles, apart from the Panthers, were as surely outclassed by the Shermans as the Luftwaffe's fighters were by the Spitfires and the Mustangs, and as its bombers were by the Lancasters and B-17s, they still had the skill, the tactical experience and, certainly, the courage to be a formidable fighting force.

Those of the tank-men who had returned from the cold, grey wastes of Russia remembered bitter battles, and costly advances which always ended in retreat; on their way to France they had passed through their homeland, and had seen the ruined cities - their cities - with streets full of rubble and smothered in dust; they had seen the townspeople - their people - treading carefully in the debris, flinching from the roar of their engines as they passed. The hardships and miseries of the Eastern Front might now be behind them, but they were soon to undergo another sort of ordeal - the sort that those townspeople already knew too well - the ordeal of heavy air attack.

CHAPTER FOUR

AIRBORNE

On that Wednesday evening, with the moon suspended above the flat horizon and with the broad expanse of Lincolnshire lying palely in its light, the silence was broken and the air began to tremble as on nineteen bomber airfields the Merlin engines roared - roared as they were started, roared as they were test-run, roared as they dragged the laden Lancasters out of the dispersals and along the narrow, winding taxi-tracks to the runway thresholds. In the towns and the villages of East and West Lindsey, of Holland and Kesteven, window-panes rattled, chinaware shook, and people turned up the volume of their wireless-sets to hear Stewart Hibberd on the BBC. They were accustomed to the din, and were able to relate it to the uniformed young men who strolled along their lanes, came to their farms for eggs "off the ration" and thronged their public houses - the young men who were making all the noise.

The Lancasters of 5 Group led the way into the air, for they would form the first wave to approach the target. At fifteen minutes to ten, Wing Commander Laurence Deane, the Officer Commanding 83 Squadron and the Main Force Controller for the operation, lifted OL D-Dog off the runway at Coningsby with a load of six red spot fires, four green TIs, three recce flares and four 1,000 pound high explosive bombs. After Deane came his deputy, Squadron Leader Neville Sparks in OL R-Robert, and twenty more Lancasters of Cochrane's own flare-force and backers-up from Nos. 83 and 97 Squadrons. "Ned" Sparks (as he was known) and his crew were embarking on the twenty-first operation of their tour.

Another experienced 83 Squadron crew was that of Flight Lieutenant Arthur Keeling, DFM, who were flying their twenty-third operation - most of them as Pathfinders - in OL J-Jig of "A" flight. Their orders on this one, as "Flares 1", were to drop their TIs when ordered by the Marker Leader, make a circuit of the target and go in again to unload their cargo of delayed-action bombs on the red spot fires. Seated in the curtained cabin compartment behind Keeling were Flight Lieutenant Chapman, DFM, the navigator, and Flying Officer Harpham, the bomb-aimer - or "air-bomber", as his role was now described in the squadron's battle order. "Hank" Harpham was twenty-seven years of age and, in civil life, had been a farmer near Sleaford, only twelve miles south-west of his base. He had set out in the Air Force with the dream of being a pilot, as had many bomb-aimers, but within a fortnight of his wings parade in Canada, at the end of a "circuits-and-bumps" detail at a relief landing field, he had considerately given the Airfield Control Pilot a lift back to base in his Oxford trainer. The fact that the aircraft carried no spare parachute had neither bothered Harpham, nor his passenger, but it had bothered his Flight Commander, who was a stickler for the rules. There had been no pilot's wings for Harpham, but a sixteen-week bombing course and a single wing instead. Now, in common with many of his colleagues, he was a qualified radar operator, and would assist Chapman with the navigation by identifying landmarks on the H2S.

As the take-offs continued at Bardney and Waddington, Dunholme Lodge and Skellingthorpe, Woodhall Spa and Spilsby, at East Kirkby, Fiskerton and Metheringham, the Lancasters of 1 Group joined the aerial armada. At Wickenby, both squadrons, observing the 'Goodwood' requirement in the operation order, had committed their full complement of serviceable aircraft: seventeen from 12 Squadron and thirteen from 626. A green light flashed from the chequered caravan which stood beside the downwind end of runway two-seven. For the next half-hour, at the rate of one a minute, Wickenby's bombers would roar down that runway, and climb into the night. PH V-Victor of 12 Squadron rolled from the taxi-track into line between the flare-path lights, halted while the pilot, First Lieutenant Dawley - a USAAF officer serving with the RAF - made his final take-off checks and, with the familiar crescendo of six-thousand horse-power from the four Rolls-Royce Merlins, moved heavily away, gradually accelerating, towards the darkness in the west.

It was not unknown for bomber crews to be high-spirited, even rumbustious; they were sometimes ill-assorted, if not incompatible. Lail K. Dawley's crew, in training, had been more boisterous, and less obviously compatible, than most. One reason for this was that they felt they had a "jinx". Dawley was their third captain in what had been, until his arrival four months earlier, an inglorious, if colourful, career. Their original captain had chosen the occasion of the crew's final flight at Lindholme HCU to suffer a nervous breakdown. For once, the crew had worked together well enough to prise him away from the controls and, more by luck than good judgement, to land the aircraft in one piece. The invalid's successor, again on the eve of finishing the course and being posted to a squadron, had suddenly decided that he wished to have no part in the bombing of "defenceless" women and children. Temporarily unhinged, perhaps, by these experiences, the crew had taken to a life of naughtiness; two of them - Flight Sergeant Allen, the bomb-aimer, and Sergeant Stephens, the mid-upper gunner - had followed this career to such effect that they had numerous charges of "conduct to the prejudice of good order and Air Force discipline" to answer. These included the impersonation of an officer, by Stephens, on a WAAF kit inspection, and the painting, by Allen, of a large "doomie" on the station parade ground.

Dawley, a married man from Michigan, who had arrived at Lindholme just in time to save the crew from further obloquy, owed his situation to his age and to his stature: the USAAC, in which he had enlisted in 1940, had regarded him as too old for fighters and too short-limbed for bombers, and he had become a temporary Canadian to find a way into the war. Having obtained his wings, he had been accepted back into what by then had become the USAAF, which promptly loaned him to the RAF; he now received as much pay as any four of his British colleagues put together, and was not subject to the King's Regulations and Air Council Instructions by which their lives were circumscribed. He differed further from previous captains of the jinx crew in that, when flying, he insisted upon carrying a loaded .45 revolver in a shoulder holster, and in that, far from suffering a breakdown or feeling qualms about his conscience, he had attempted - unsuccessfully - to loop the loop in the Lancaster on their final training flight.

The crew's tour at Wickenby had begun, on the night of their arrival, with the last operation of the Berlin campaign, on which Dawley had flown his "second-dickey trip" while his crew filled vacancies in other pilots' aircraft. The tour had continued with such targets as Stuttgart, Schweinfurt and Augsburg. By 3rd May, the jinx was far behind them: they had completed fifteen missions, and only the crew of Pilot Officer Black, RCAF, stood ahead as the senior surviving squadron crew. After the briefing for Mailly-le-Camp, Dawley had confided his own tactical plan. "Listen, you guys. This is a milk-run, and we'll have some fun. What we do, we make the bomb-run, then we go down real low and shoot the shit outa the sons of bitches." With keen anticipation, the crew had climbed aboard V-Victor and taken their positions.

Close behind V-Victor in the line for take-off came three more 12 Squadron aircraft: PH C-Charlie with Pilot Officer Black and the senior crew, PH Z-Zebra with Flying Officer Ormrod at the controls, and PH Q-Queenie with Flying Officer Maxwell, who had made the critical report about the Special Duty Flight's marking on the last operation, and who, with fourteen operations, was Dawley's nearest rival in the seniority race (it was an amicable rivalry: the NCOs of both crews shared a Nissen hut).

From the flight briefing, three hours earlier, Peter Maxwell had gathered that he was taking part in a limited attack on a military target, and that, in the interests of accuracy, the bombs were to be dropped from a lower height than usual. The Met. man had given a good weather forecast - hardly any cloud and a three-quarter moon - and the SIO had described the target defences as minimal. Compared with some of his recent operations, Mailly-le-Camp hadn't sounded all that formidable - nor should it, he told himself, since it was only to count as one third of a mission. Had it been a full one, he would, by tomorrow, have been half-way through his tour. Anyway, he felt fairly happy about it: he missed his old favourite, Z-Zebra (the crew who had taken her to Nuremberg on 30th March had failed to bring her back, and the new Z-Zebra was in other hands), but Q-Queenie seemed a nice enough kite to fly, and he had his regular, familiar crew: Sergeant Crighton, the flight engineer, sat beside him, Flight Lieutenant Garlick was navigating, Sergeant O'Hara was at the bomb-sight, Sergeant Lloyd at the big Marconi wireless-set, and Sergeants Davidson and Townsend were manning the gun-turrets. He made a slow, left-hand circuit over Wickenby, and settled down to climb on course for Beachy Head. That was a far safer way to gain operational height than making upward spirals over Lincolnshire among another three hundred Lancasters, all of which were doing the same. In cloud or in darkness, that could be almost as hazardous as flying across the defences of Berlin.

Away into the night, following Q-Queenie, went 12 Squadron's P-Peter with Pilot Officer Thompson at the controls, and then came a succession of 626 Squadron's aircraft: Flight Sergeant Bladon flying UM E-Easy Two, then Pilot Officer Carter in UM H-Howe, Flight Sergeant Dyer-Matthews in UM F-Fox and Flight Sergeant Carroll in UM B-Baker. Carroll's crew were also half-way through their tour - a tour which had included the bad night over Nuremberg five weeks earlier when ninety-six were lost and nine more written off. Twice in the last few ops they had been attacked by night-fighters, and each time a burst from the mid-upper gunner, Sergeant Bert Garlick (who was no relation to Maurice Garlick in Maxwell's Q-Queenie), and violent corkscrews by Carroll had got them out of trouble. Garlick, however, had his own little trouble, and that was Sergeant Lawrence, the crew's wireless-operator. Bill Lawrence was a widower from Durham, with two small children and an uncertain temper. Given two pints of bitter on a crew outing, he became overwhelmed by an urge to punch somebody's nose, and the nose he favoured was invariably Garlick's. In the course of their tour, therefore, Garlick, an easy-going Yorkshireman, twenty-one years old, who preferred to do his fighting with two Browning guns, had become as expert as his pilot in evasive action.

B-Baker was followed down the runway by Pilot Officer Jackson in UM Z-Zebra Two and then by Flying Officer Butcher in UM K-King Two. John Butcher was flying the twenty-second mission of a tour which had begun with the Battle of Berlin; indeed, at the start of the campaign, his bomb-aimer, Flying Officer George Wilson, had hardly unpacked his kit on arriving at Wickenby before being called on to deputise for a temporarily absent member of your author's crew. Having survived the Big City battle, Butcher and his crew had reached the stage where, if they were careful and if Lady Luck stayed with them, they should have been looking forward, in two or three weeks' time, to a small celebration and their end-of-tour leave. The recent edict about French targets had jeopardised that prospect, and Wilson, for one, wasn't altogether pleased. He had been happy enough when the Command was diverted to pre-invasion targets, welcoming the chance, for the first time in his tour, to aim his bombs from less than 20,000 feet, but the "third of an op" rule had come as a quite a blow. "It undermined our faith in the leadership," he commented later, "to find that they could change the rules that governed our lives."

For the two 626 Squadron crews who were next in the take-off line - Pilot Officer Ayres' in UM M-Mike Two and Pilot Officer Fisher's in UM S-Sugar Two - their tours seemed to stretch far ahead into the future, for they were just beginning their operational careers. The members of both crews had friends in the other, and the two navigators - Sergeants Denzil Ede and Noel Hatton - who had been on the same initial training course, were particularly close. Bob Ayres, by a few weeks the senior of the two pilots, had made a secret, unofficial compact to call Norman Fisher on the base RT frequency, when the aircraft were crossing the Channel on the homeward route, with a brief enquiry as to how things were in Sugar Two.

As the two "sprog" crews climbed away into the night, they were followed by a veteran. Flight Lieutenant Wright, on a green from the caravan, opened the throttles of 626's UM C-Charlie Two and moved off the taxi-track onto the runway. Tony Wright, with his straggling moustache, battered peaked cap and faded SD uniform, could have served as a model for a Hooper cartoon in "Tee Emm" magazine (he eschewed battle-dress on the grounds that he didn't wish to look scruffy if, by misadventure, he should land away from base), and his unquenchable thirst had, in months past, shocked your author's abstemious rear gunner, whose strong belief it was that alcohol and flying were incompatible. Wright, in defiance of that view, was now within two operations - two whole operations - of the end of his tour.

Charlie Two was followed by a cluster of 12 Squadron aircraft: PH O-Orange, PH K-King and PH D-Dog; then came Flight Sergeant Barkway in 626 Squadron's UM D-Dog Two and Flight Lieutenant Breckenridge in UM X-ray Two. Bill Breckenridge was flying his twelfth operation, but not with all the crew that he had started out with: there had been casualties on their sixth trip when, running in to drop the bomb-load on Berlin, he was bounced by a fighter and had been lucky to survive. He, his navigator, Pilot Officer Meek, RCAF, and both gunners had been wounded, and his wireless operator killed. The passage home to a forced landing on the Norfolk coast had been a desperate endeavour, recognised by the award of the DFC to Breckenridge and to his mid-upper gunner, Pilot Officer Biff Baker of the RCAF. Jack Meek, then an NCO, had won the CGM - a rare award indeed.

The last 12 Squadron aircraft to take off - PH L-Love, flown by Flight Lieutenant Gray - left the ground at ten minutes past ten, and one young Canadian was glad to see it go. Leading Aircraftman Greg Biefer, radar mechanic, twenty-two years old, had started work on the dispersals at 8.45 that morning, servicing the Gee boxes and the H2S sets in all the squadron aircraft. Any major defect meant a dash across the airfield to fetch a replacement unit from the radar section. His lunch had been a "wad" from the NAAFI van with a mug of tea, and his task had lasted until six-thirty in the evening. He had cycled to the Airmens' Mess for supper, and found a message on the notice board: "LAC Biefer, report for Section Guard Duty, 1930 hours." It was signed by his senior NCO. Queueing at the counter for his sausages and beans, he had pondered on the fate that had brought him to Wickenby and set him under a Flight Sergeant - a fellow Canadian - who, for whatever reason, had disliked him on sight. This Section Guard Duty, for which he knew he had been detailed far more often than his colleagues, included a time-consuming chore known as "detting", which consisted of touring the dispersals and connecting each aircraft's IFF equipment to its detonator circuit. (The IFF - "identification friend or foe" - transponder gave protection, in theory, against unfortunate mistakes by the fighters and AA gunners of the ADGB; the explosive charge was detonated automatically if the aircraft crashed, and could be triggered by the crew if they made a forced landing in hostile territory). The aircrews had been arriving at dispersal, and preparing to emplane, by the time Biefer had finished putting in the plugs. First thing next morning, he would visit the dispersals on a "de-detting" tour, and hope that the cooks would save him a late breakfast.

Greg Biefer (2nd from left) with another radar mechanic (1st left), and four of the crew of 12 Sqn's S-sugar: Pilot Officer Pollard from Trinidad (Captain), Sergeant Reneau (Wireless Op), Sergeant Alberry (Flight Engineer) and Flight Sergeant Wettlaufer, RCAF (Navigator). The crew took part in the attack; the aircraft with Pollard and Wettlaufer were lost on 30 June/1 July.

At Binbrook and at Kirmington, the scene at Wickenby was being replicated, as it was at Killingholme and Ludford, Elsham Wolds and Kelstern. (According to the orders, it should have been the same at Faldingworth, where four Lancasters of 1 Group's Polish squadron, No. 300, were to have joined the operation. That none did is certain: the reason why is not.)

On Kirmington's battle order, the rear gunner in 166 Squadron's AS B-Baker, flown by Flying Officer Warmington, was listed as Sergeant Petersen. This was, in fact, the nom de guerre of a twenty-two year-old Dane, Andreas Petersen Moldt. As a cadet in the Danish Merchant Navy, Moldt had been in mid-Atlantic en route to America when the war began and, having served his cadetship, he had sailed to Britain in the convoys, through the U-boats and the storms, until he had decided, in 1942, that he had acquired sufficient mastery of the English language to join the fighting forces. He had made his way to Montreal, and joined the RCAF. At half-past nine in the evening of 3rd May 1944, Andreas Moldt, now known as Andy Petersen, found himself sitting in a turret at the back end of a Lancaster, about to embark upon his first operation. Forty years later, in an account of his life, both as seaman and air gunner, he was to write these words about that day:

"We were not senior enough to have our own Lancaster, so we borrowed B-Baker as its crew was on leave. It was nearly new from the factory. Supper was at 1700 hours and briefing at 1800. The building where this took place had a large room where the far wall had a detailed map of Europe. After being checked in by the RAF Police, the first thing we did was to look at the red line showing the track for the night's operation. It led to a small town with the name of Mailly-le-Camp. Here, the Germans had a training camp for their Tiger tanks and also reserves of tanks and transport vehicles of an unknown strength.

Ivon and John - captain and navigator - met before the rest of us for a special briefing. Instructions were then given by the different sections: bomb load, petrol; and marking of the target by TIs green followed by red spot markers. The Master Bomber would then give a short order on VHF where to bomb in relation to the red markers. The briefing continued with information about the German defences and what we could expect: flak along the route, night fighters at the various aerodromes, etc. the radio operators were instructed on their contact with Group HQ.

Two of our worst enemies were characterised by the number 88 - the twin-engined Junkers 88 and the Fliegerabwehrkanone 88 mm (designated Flak by us). In addition, there were the Messerschmitt 110 and the single-engined Focke Wulf 190. The latter were not ground-controlled but flew free-lance - we called them 'Cats-eye people'. When there were searchlights but no flak above a target we were to expect a swarm of them around. The pilots were known for their contempt of death in their daring flights in and around the bomber stream.

After briefing, we received the bag with money (today it was French) and our escape kit, and after picking up our flying kit we went by crew-bus to our aircraft. Each aircraft had a permanent ground crew of three men - rigger, fitter and mechanic - who helped each other, ignoring trade limits.

The waiting time before take-off was passed in a small hut made by the ground crew out of bits and pieces they had found. Here we sat chatting until it was time to get ready. Bill, the mid-upper, and I had to start before the others - first the electrically-heated inner suit and inner boots, then the yellow outer flying suit, which we called the 'Canary' suit, flying boots and harness. The helmet and gloves were put on after getting into our turrets. The outer suit was fireproof, could not sink and small pieces of shrapnel would not pierce it. Then came the helmet with oxygen mask and microphone, which was electrically-heated to prevent damage by moisture. Next came four pairs of gloves - first silk, then woollen mittens, then the electrically-heated ones connected to two terminals on the inner suit, and finally the long leather gauntlets. Only the forehead was exposed to the air, as the perspex had been cut away to prevent oil from the two inner engines being blown onto it and hindering the rear gunner's view. So there was a lot of fresh air. The worst part was getting into all this equipment on a warm summer evening and avoiding perspiring.

Five minutes before we have to taxi out, we get into our seats. Just outside my turret on the port side was the holder for my parachute, and I secure it before entering the turret, feet first, and then closing the sliding doors, oxygen connection on, intercom connected and tested, and also the tumbler switch on my controls. It was placed there so that I did not have to take my hands off the gun controls when I had to use the microphone. Now I am ready. Oxygen and electrical heating are turned on after take-off. With the helmet on, the sound from the four Merlins is not so very loud. Then we start rolling out of our 'frying-pan', along the perimeter track to the end of the runway - the length of which is about 2,000 metres. After the green from the caravan, we taxi to the take-off position and the skipper

straightens up the aircraft. With the brakes on, the inner engines
are revved up, brakes off, and we start rolling. The outer engines
are revved up and used to keep the aircraft straight and we are
gaining speed rapidly. I can feel the tailwheel is off the ground
and I am several metres in the air. I can feel corrections on the
rudders as small sideways jerks. It takes us nearly the whole
length of the runway even though we are not at maximum weight
tonight. The period is critical: if we get engine trouble during
these seconds, a belly landing is inevitable. We are airborne at
2150 hours."

Nineteen minutes after Laurence Deane had taken off from Coningsby,
and the sound of the Lancasters had all but died away, Wing Commander
Cheshire, three miles to the north, turned his Mark VI Mosquito onto the
runway at Woodhall Spa and took off in pursuit. Close beside him in the tiny,
cramped cockpit of AJ N-Nan sat his regular navigator, Flying Officer Pat
Kelly. Of Cheshire's pilots, Squadron Leader Dave Shannon was designated
first deputy; he and his navigator, Flying Officer Len Sumpter, were already in
the air in Mosquito AJ L-Love and closing on the Lancasters. It was they who,
with Cheshire, would initiate the marking on the west end of the target.
Shannon's operations now tallied over sixty, Cheshire's many more: neither
man was counting. The second and third deputies - Flight Lieutenant Kearns
of the RNZAF and Flight Lieutenant Fawke - who were to mark the second
aiming-point, followed their leader fifteen minutes later in Mosquitos AJ S-
Sugar and AJ M-Mike. Dave Kearns and his navigator, Flying Officer Barclay
(another New Zealander) were flying their third tour together: they had started
out on Wellingtons and had been early Pathfinders. Gerry Fawke and Flying
Officer Bennett were also highly experienced. If the outcome of the Mailly-le-
Camp operation could only have depended on the skill and the courage of such
veterans as these, all might have yet gone well on that May night. But the
demon seeds were sown, and nothing could prevent their deadly growth.

For the crew of Wickenby's PH Q-Queenie, the first two hours of the
flight were uneventful. The aircraft cruised smoothly across the Channel and
the coast of France before Maxwell banked into an eastward turn towards the
target. For once, he decided, the met. man had got the weather right: the sky
was clear, and moonlight glinted on the rivers and threw the shadows of the
copses on the scene below. Maxwell glanced at Crighton, and chuckled as he
remembered the engineer's expression, back in the dispersal-pan, when two
Land Army girls had stopped on the track beside the perimeter-fence to wave

and wish them luck. "Jinxes," Crighton had muttered as he turned away, and O'Hara had agreed. A superstitious lot, the Scots and the Irish, thought Maxwell. He was a hard-headed Midlander, and had no time for that sort of nonsense. Besides, the girls had looked rather nice.

"Pilot from navigator."

"Go ahead."

"ETA at the target is zero-zero-eighteen. Your course and airspeed are OK."

"Roger, Nav."

By this time, for two of Wickenby's crews, the Mailly-le-Camp operation was already over, and both were back at base. After climbing to 8,000 feet, the pilot of 12 Squadron's PH O-Oboe, Flight Sergeant Richardson, had found that two of his main blind-flying instruments were giving false readings and the others none at all. Deciding that the mission had to be abandoned, he flew sixty miles out over the North Sea and, to reduce O-Oboe's weight to the maximum for landing, jettisoned the "cookie" and nine of the 500-pounders into the black expanse below. In 626 Squadron's UM J-Jig Two, Pilot Officer Bennett, RCAF, had embarked on the thirteenth operation of a tour which had included Schweinfurt, Berlin, both Stuttgart and Frankfurt twice, and the bad one to Nuremberg. Amongst these, he had already experienced two abortive sorties and, not wanting any more, had been sickened to the heart when, half an hour after take-off, with the aircraft on course over Bedfordshire at 10,000 feet, flames had trailed back from the starboard outer engine. More profligate than Richardson, Bennett had dropped the whole load in the sea. Nor had his misfortunes ended there: in a final touch of bathos, returning to the billets after the de-briefing, J-Jig Two's navigator had fallen off his bicycle and fractured an arm.

Abortive sorties were anathema to all: to aircrew, ground crew and every commander up to the AOC. Air Chief-Marshal Harris didn't care for them, either. If a crew aborted with any sort of frequency, people began to look at them askance, as though the problems which had caused them to turn back might be more in their minds than in the aeroplane's machinery. Neither Richardson nor Bennett, however, could be faulted for their actions: with his instruments malfunctioning (probably due to ice in the pitot or the static tubes), Richardson could not have flown accurately enough to make the bombing run, while the power to drive Bennett's mid-upper turret had gone when an internal coolant leak caused the fire in his starboard outer engine.

Six aircraft altogether made "early returns" - four from No. 1 Group and two (including one Mosquito of 627 Squadron) from No. 5 Group. Thus marginally depleted, the bomber stream flew on, and the German radars were following its course. At listening posts in Britain, the voice of the night-fighter controller came through clearly: "Bombers are approaching the Amiens zone" and, a little later, "Bombers are entering the Beauvais zone". The responses, too, were monitored: pilots of I Gruppe NJG 4 at Florennes, and of II Gruppe at Coulommiers, were orbiting their beacons and waiting for instructions.

Unknown to those pilots, the specially-trained "Elint" operators in 192 Squadron's Halifaxes, some five thousand feet above the bomber stream, were watching out for them. In DT V-Victor, piloted by Flight Sergeant Harry Gibson, Flying Officer Munro was busy at his receiver, searching the ether in the UHF range for the signals that would tell him that a night-fighter's AI radar was in use. V-Victor's bomb-aimer, Warrant Officer Elder, with no bombs to aim, would assist Sergeant Preece, the navigator, in plotting the positions where Munro's electronic intelligence was gathered, and would man the front guns if they should be required. Sergeants Stormont, Ackroyd, Nicholson and Burton, respectively the wireless operator, flight engineer, mid-upper and rear gunners, were at their normal stations and, as V-Victor was equipped with a rare mid-under firing point, Sergeant Cottrell was manning a 0.5 inch Browning on a ball-mounting in the floor of the fuselage, at the point where, in most British heavies, the H2S scanner's housing was located. Cyril Cottrell and Sergeant Jim Carpenter, friends since enrolment and both fresh out of training, had that very day been cleared for operations, and it had been a toss-up as to which of them would fly and which would go on leave.

One of Cottrell's kitbags had been lost in transit and, when it fell to him to fly the operation, he had borrowed Carpenter's flying clothes before he climbed aboard V-Victor.

Leonard Cheshire, who flew a Mosquito in much the same manner as, in his youth, he had driven a succession of high-powered motor cars, arrived over Mailly-le-Camp eight minutes earlier than he had intended. Anxious not to alert the defences of the depot and send the Panzertruppen scurrying to shelter, he sought out the night-fighter base at St. Dizier, some nineteen miles away, and, assuming the guise of an intruder, buzzed around it noisily until his scheduled ETA on target came up on the clock. By then, a PFF Mosquito, high

Seargeant Cotrell, Air Gunner in a Halifax of 192 Sqn's DT-V

above on its Oboe run, was within seconds of "Release".

Shannon and Sumpter, in 617's AJ L-Love, had also been a little early, and had flown a few dog-legs to bring them in on time. At one minute after midnight, Sumpter checked his Gee-box. "We're there, Dave," he said, "but where are the Oboe flares?" No sooner had he spoken, than the PFF illuminator lighted up the scene, and Cheshire's red spot fires followed seconds later. Shannon held off, flying figures of eight at 3,500 feet, until he heard his leader's order to "come in". Diving steeply at the brightly burning marker, he released his own red spot fires from four hundred feet (he later reported, at the Woodhall Spa de-briefing, that his markers had fallen slightly west of centre). The time was exactly 0006 hours - H-hour plus five - which was right on the limit of his time-band for marking. Shannon made a wide circuit of the area and waited for the onslaught to begin.

CHAPTER FIVE

ON TARGET

Flying Officer Saint-Smith, piloting a Mosquito of 627 Squadron, had marked the assembly-point south-west of Châlons-sur-Marne with two yellow spot fires at 0001 hours - exactly on schedule - and the pilots of the leading 5 Group Lancasters, complying with the orders, were making orbits round them. Laurence Deane, approaching in the van of 83 Squadron, had seen the markers fall. Thirty years later, he was to set down his recollections of the scene:

"At precisely zero minus five, the clear moonlit sky was transformed by a warm yellow glow as the parachute flares were released. I tilted my aircraft over to port to gain a better view of the ground; immediately below, the barrack buildings stood out in relief. Within seconds, or so it seemed, a large red glow appeared - Cheshire had located the aiming point and marked it by dropping a red spot fire. He called me over the RT, we agreed the accuracy of the marker and I instructed my wireless-operator to inform the bombing force to attack."

Cheshire's description of this phase differs slightly in the timing and in the number of markers which were burning on the ground. "At zero hour," he was to write in his report, "the aiming point was accurately marked and equally accurately backed-up by the Deputy. Orders were immediately passed to the Main Force Controller to start bombing." (For Cheshire, H-hour or zero-hour meant a minute past midnight - 0001 hours - which accorded with the plan, while for Deane it seems to have meant either three minutes earlier or five minutes later, depending on the context.)

The Bomber Command Night Raid Report, classified as secret, provides a remarkable variant: "Marking on the SE aiming-point was abortive; one set of TIs failed to explode, and the other Mosquito was intercepted by a fighter." Just how this information gained credence is impossible to tell: Cheshire, Deane and Shannon - the leading participants - recall no such occurrence. Whatever its origin, the matter in itself is not of great consequence: the following events were very much more serious, for it was then that the seeds sown in the planning began to show their buds. Again, there were variations between the official report of the events and the way the main participants later related them, but the story was basically the same. "Unfortunately," Cheshire would state in his report next morning, "the Controller's communications were not satisfactory, and a delay of five minutes ensued before he passed on his message." Deane, it transpired, believing that the 5 Group force were occupying the air-space between four and six thousand feet, decided to fly a thousand feet below them.

"I felt elated that everything had gone so perfectly, and reflected on the havoc that any minute would be wreaked on that peaceful, sleeping camp. I checked with my navigator, who advised it was zero hour, yet nothing was happening; Mailly-le-Camp just glowed in the light of the single red marker. My elation changed to concern: where were the three hundred-plus bombing aircraft? I checked again. It was zero plus two and not a bomb had been dropped. My wireless operator confirmed that he had sent out the bombing instructions and was repeating them continually. I called up Neville Sparks, my deputy, who likewise was mystified over the absence of bombs. Something had gone wrong - but what?"

What had gone wrong was partially described in the subsequent Form 540 - the Operations Record Book - compiled at St. Vincents by the 5 Group Headquarters staff: "The marking was prompt and accurate, but unfortunately RT communication was badly interrupted by an RT station broadcasting American news, and the WT transmitter in the leader's aircraft was at least 30 kilocycles off frequency."

The incident of the American broadcast is just one more mystery in the story of the mission. It was heard, and reported, by many main force pilots (although a few of them, and Deane himself, described it as a British news broadcast), but whether it resulted from a radio counter-measure by the enemy defences, employing a recording, or from an unfortunate clash of frequencies, cannot be determined. The latter alternative is more probable because, as will be remembered, two US Armies were then based in Britain, preparing for "Overlord", and, wherever the US Army went, it tended to establish a radio facility, with a high-powered transmitter, dedicated to reminding the GIs, by the sound of such well-loved performers as Bing Crosby, Glenn Miller and Dinah Shore, and by the Stateside news, of what they were fighting for.

"It was evident," Deane would write in his later account, "that the instructions relayed by my wireless operator had not been received by the majority, and I had no other means of communicating with them." In this, he over-estimated the numbers receiving his WT transmissions, which no-one heard at all, and under-estimated his ability to reach them by RT. He could hear the pilots - "The order that RT silence should be maintained was now being broken from all quarters," he would write, "and the gist of the many messages addressed to me, some orderly but many crudely blunt, was to enquire when they could bomb and get the hell out" - and yet did not, in recollection, accept the fact that he could talk to them. In this, he believed that he was adhering to his briefing - to keep RT silence and pass his orders to the main force by WT.

Deane's recollection, however, does not equate with the report he made at de-briefing as recorded in the 83 Squadron Form 541 - the Operations Record Book - which included numerous references to his use of the RT to communicate with the main force. This inconsistency between the immediate report and the recall of events after more than three decades is entirely understandable: it would indeed be remarkable if the two were totally consistent. Furthermore, Forms 541 cannot be regarded as repositories of eternal truths. Your author, reading what purport to be his own raid reports as retained in the archives of the Public Record Office, has at times been unable to recognise the content. The reports, after all, from which the forms were compiled were often hastily written in the early morning hours by weary de-briefing officers doing their best to summarise the remarks of even wearier crews.

At 0010 hours, the first wave's attack on the east end of the target, which should by then have been nearing its completion, had only just begun. That it began at all was probably due to a combination of initiatives. Some 5 Group pilots (and a 1 Group pilot of 460 Squadron who either misread the time or chose to promote himself to the first wave), reaching the assembly-point, saw the red spot fires on the ground to the south and decided to attack, whereupon others, observing the unmistakable flashes of the detonating bombs and of the photo-flares, simply followed suit. Deane accepts this latter possibility, without being entirely sure of how it came to happen: "It was now zero plus eight…" (for Cheshire and the planners this was H-hour plus thirteen) "…and fortunately at this stage the bombs already bursting on the target were accepted as sufficient signal for all to bomb without waiting for specific instructions."

The other, more laudable, initiative was that of Squadron Leader Sparks who, realising that Deane's message wasn't getting through, himself called in the more punctilious pilots, first by WT, and then by simply talking through the interference on the RT. Within the next five minutes, some sixty Lancasters made their bombing runs. Three hundred and twenty tons of high-explosive fell upon the depot of Mailly-le-Camp, and Len Sumpter, sitting by Dave Shannon in Mosquito AJ L-Love, watched them fall. "The initial bombing," he told your author later, "seemed to be well in the vicinity of the red spots, so we wended our way home."

However initiated, the attack began well. "The bombing, when it started," Cheshire would report, "was accurate and reasonably concentrated and appeared to be producing the desired results. While it was in progress, the second and third deputies arrived on the scene and stood by to mark the Western aiming point for the second wave."

That second wave - the main body of the 1 Group complement - was now nearing the assembly-point, where the original yellow spot fires had burned out and had been reinforced by Flight Lieutenant DeVigne of 627 Squadron. As for the "special target" force of Rice's embryo markers and the small band of heavies, whose attack by now, according to the plan, should have been completed, their part in the operation appears to have remained a secret to all but the planners and themselves. Certainly, the efforts of the SD Flight and the "1 Group Controller" went unnoticed by Cheshire and by Deane. The latter, indeed, denies their very existence: "The carrying and dropping of markers was sacrosanct," he wrote. "Even experienced crews on first joining the Pathfinder Force weren't entrusted with markers until they had qualified by a number of trips as trainees. I can't believe therefore that any crew in 1 Group had marking responsibilities - nor that 1 Group had its own Controller. Certainly as Master Bomber for the raid I wasn't so informed. You can't have two bosses on anything so important as a bombing raid!"

Deane sturdily rejects the whole concept, not only of a "special target", but that there were different aiming points in the depot site. "With the

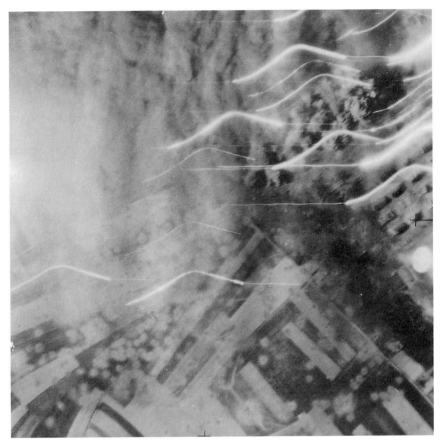

Flash photograph taken over the target by an attacking Lancaster.

inevitable bombing errors," he argued, "the whole small area would have been obliterated by 300 plus heavy bomb loads with just one aiming point." As to that, it would be hard to disagree with the Wing Commander's judgement. Nevertheless, the crews of the special target force did their best to carry out their task. The first green spot fire, which went down a little earlier than planned, undershot the target by about a thousand yards; the second, some time later, fell four hundred yards away - an inadequate improvement. Tensely, the captains and the bomb-aimers listened for their orders. At last they heard the voice of the SD Flight leader: "Firepump Two from Firepump One. I am hit, and going down." The voice was calm and unhurried: the message was his last. His deputy, satisfied that a third green spot fire had fallen close to the aiming-point, tried to call the bombers in. By now, however, another instruction was coming through the headphones: "All aircraft, bomb - aim at the reds." In all probability, the voice was that of Neville Sparks, addressing the main force, but, acting on the old Service maxim that the last order you receive is the one that you obey, the special force pilots turned their aircraft towards "the reds" on the main depot target. Of the few captains who, through the RT cacophony, failed to hear that order, and attacked the "special target", two felt sure that they almost hit the aiming-point.

Leading the 5 Group force were the twenty-one Lancasters of Nos. 97 and 83 Squadrons. The general opinion among the pilots of these aircraft, whose duty lay in backing up the markers, tended to support Leonard Cheshire's impression that the initial aiming point was receiving accurate attention. Operating the wireless set in one of 97 Squadron's aircraft was Sergeant Frank Broughton, a twenty-two year old Yorkshireman, who was engaged in what was actually his second operation, but his first since the squadron had moved to Coningsby from Bourn and, furthermore, his first with the young Flying Officer who was piloting the aircraft. As a new crew, they were not carrying marker-flares, as were their more experienced colleagues, but a full load of one-thousand pound bombs.

Broughton's recollection of the briefing was that the barracks must be bombed at ten minutes after midnight, so that the troops - he believes he was told that they were all SS men - would be fast asleep in bed. His own instructions were to listen out, as usual, every half-hour on the Group WT frequency and to record whatever message he received, which might include information about the winds found en route by selected leading navigators, the weather back at base and possible diversions. He was scrupulous in this, not only for his crew's sake, but because each broadcast included a particular, different numeral which had to be recorded in his log; any default would bring down on him the wrath of the Squadron Signals Leader. There had been nothing in the briefing which caused him to expect that the Main Force Controller's orders would be broadcast on WT.

Over the target, Broughton slid out of his seat and stood up beside it to look out of the astrodome. Within the next few minutes, he counted six vast explosions in his immediate vicinity, and realised that Lancasters were being blown to pieces as he watched. "By heck," he ruminated, "this is a bit rough", and went back to his seat. Forty-five years later, staring into the fireplace of the tiny cottage high in the Yorkshire dales where he, as a widower, now lives alone, he seemed to be remembering the feelings he had then. "We didn't have any trouble, though," he said, "we didn't shoot at anybody, and no-one shot at us."

Like the other main force 5 Group pilots, those of 44 Squadron had expected to hear their instructions on the VHF; most of them heard nothing, and bombed when the others did; many of No. 50 Squadron's pilots, hearing only the American news broadcast on channel "C", did the same. Of 9 Squadron's pilots, most of whom heard the bombing orders retrospectively, one saw a vivid green flare at 0023 hours, which no-one else reported and which was probably one of the 1 Group SD Flight's markers aimed at the "special target". An Australian Squadron Leader of 467 Squadron, who should have known better, tried to call a colleague - a compatriot on 463 Squadron at Waddington whom he knew was on the mission - merely to make some sort of friendly contact. Another voice, which he believed to be that of the Controller but which was probably the deputy's, asked what he was up to. "Just testing," said the gregarious Australian. "Then don't," he was sharply instructed, "and get off the air". A more disciplined pilot, of 467 Squadron, reported on return to Waddington: "A good trip. I think our PFF was bang-on, just slightly late."

The crews who had the best view of the early bombing were probably those of six free-ranging 627 Squadron Mosquitos (of the ten who had set out, one returned early with an over-heating engine, and the task of the other three was to maintain the marking of the assembly-point). The six remaining pilots made themselves useful when the light flak guns around the camp perimeter opened fire on the Lancasters. Flight Lieutenant Grey of the RNZAF dropped four five-hundred pounders on a gun emplacement two miles to the east and hit it with the fourth; Flying Officer Thomson, on his second run, silenced a gun-post to the south, and Sergeant Marshallsay knocked out another at the first attempt.

By 0016 hours, as will be remembered, the first wave of heavies should have passed, and 617 Squadron's Mosquitos should have had a clear run to mark the second wave's aiming point. In fact, almost two-thirds of the first wave had yet to make their bombing runs. Cheshire, however, had no means of knowing this. Accordingly, he called Deane and told him to broadcast a direction for the attack to be suspended "so that the re-marking can be carried out." In his report, next morning, Cheshire was to write: "This order, however, was not executed, and the bombing never ceased."

Kearns and Fawke, meanwhile, were flying at 4,000 feet five miles south of the target. They heard Cheshire's message on their own RT channel, and manoeuvred their Mosquitos into position to make their marking runs, as soon as the bomb-loads ceased to fall, from south to north on the west wing of the barracks, which was fleetingly distinguishable through the billowing smoke.

Deane, being unaware, as it would seem, of any second aiming point, quite misunderstood Cheshire's reference to "re-marking". This, he took to mean a reinforcement of the first red spot fires, whereas Cheshire intended a new set of markers on the western aiming point. Not that the misunderstanding mattered very much: it merely provides another instance of the incomplete awareness of the tactical plan. Be that as it may, whichever aiming point was supposed to be marked - or re-marked - there was still a requirement for the bombing to stop while the Mosquitos made their runs across the target, and Deane, backed up by Sparks, did indeed broadcast the cease-bombing order, many times. Sparks's wireless operator constantly transmitted it on WT, while Sparks himself repeated it on RT. A number of pilots would later recall that they heard him intermittently, calling "Do not bomb yet - wait!" Deane's wireless operator was still broadcasting the right dots and dashes on the wrong frequency, while Deane, to credit the report of his post-raid de-briefing and to set aside, for the moment, his later recollection, was trying to pass the order over the RT and, indeed, at 0016 hours, by firing a red Very light. This last device, normally accepted by captains of aircraft as a signal from someone in control not to do what they were doing or appeared to be about to do, would, in that kaleidoscopic scene, lit by explosions of every description, have equated with a pin-drop in a thunderstorm, a hiccough in a hurricane.

Deane does not now recall his attempts to halt the bombing, nor was he to mention them in his subsequent account.

"The original red marker," he would write, "had almost burnt out and I headed for the aiming point to put down a fresh one. To ensure being clear of the main bombing force we approached well below them at 2,000 feet, calculated to be a 'safe' height with the 2,000 pound bombs we were told at briefing the bombing aircraft would be carrying. Never have I had such a rough flight in a Lancaster: it did everything but stand upright on its tail as each stick of bombs exploded beneath us. No wonder, as I discovered later that the aircraft of 1 Group were dropping 4,000 pounders, for which the 'safe' height was 4,000 feet. From 2,000 feet the devastation of Mailly-le-Camp was very apparent, yet approximately a further hundred Lancasters had still to shed their contribution to the destruction. It was like an inferno in Technicolor."

In fact, it was nearer to 300 than 100 aircraft which had yet to make "their contribution". Furthermore, every aircraft which had bombed and every one waiting - apart from those of Deane's own squadron and of No. 97 - carried a 4,000 pounder in its load. As for the 1 Group aircraft, all but a handful were still circling the assembly-point. Deane himself, according to the 83 Squadron Form 541, dropped four 1,000 pound bombs on the target and took the pyrotechnics back to base. It was a 97 Squadron pilot, Flying Officer Edwards, who later reinforced the second set of markers with a bomb-bay full of red spot fires.

Cheshire, meanwhile, had been in a quandary: the two aiming points had been selected for a reason, however recondite, and it was not in his remit to change the plan in flight; nevertheless, although Kearns and Fawke were in the offing and ready to mark the western aiming point, he was - willy-nilly - coming round to Deane's opinion that three hundred bomb-loads, falling reasonably close to the initial markers, would more than suffice to do the job. Furthermore, the 1 Group crews were waiting and, as he circled the target, he could tell they were in trouble. "The dense clouds of smoke," he would report, "over the whole area made an accurate marking run impossible. I instructed the Controller to order the second wave to bomb the existing marker. It was obvious that the inaccuracy of bombing which was developing and which was equally distributed over the entire target did not warrant a fresh marker. The Controller, however, would not pass the order on, and so in view of the fierce air battle which had already developed overhead, I ordered the second and third deputies to re-mark the aiming point in spite of the heavy bombing which was still in progress."

If Deane heard those instructions to bring the 1 Group force in on the original aiming-point, he neither referred to them later nor remembers them now. In any event, in view of his incomplete awareness understanding of the Marker Leader's plan, he would have either found them incomprehensible or judged that they had been overtaken by the progress of events.

So, while Deane was flying across the target through the shock waves of the "cookies", and while Edwards of 97 Squadron was approaching with his pyrotechnic cargo, Kearns and Fawke were diving on the depot from 5,000 feet to mark the second aiming point. According to the plan, they should have been on target at H-hour plus 11 (twelve minutes after midnight, or 0012 hours); Fawke, in fact, dropped his four red spot fires from 2,000 feet at 0023 hours, and Kearns dropped his from a thousand feet higher at 0025. Dave Kearns told your author later of the moments that followed: "I had just released my markers, checked 'bombs gone' and bomb-doors closed, when a bomb-load including a 4,000 pounder exploded in front of me. I don't recall the next few seconds clearly other than bright flashes, severe turbulence and the Mosquito being thrown all over the sky. When I regained control we were some three miles to the north of the target. I checked that my navigator was uninjured and that the aircraft was responding normally. Bombs were still falling on the target area as we set course for Woodhall Spa."

If the blast of the "cookies" at 4,000 feet had tossed Deane's thirty-ton Lancaster about and given him his roughest-ever ride, it must have treated the Mosquito, a quarter of the weight and a thousand feet lower, to a fearful shaking. A less skilful pilot, in a less robust aircraft, might not have made the journey back to Woodhall Spa.

Not surprisingly, neither Fawke nor Kearns was entirely content with the result of their efforts: they reported at de-briefing that the first set of markers fell on the north-western corner of the depot site, and the second on the north-eastern corner. The northern edge of the target, therefore, was well-marked: the western side, which should have been the second wave's aiming point, was not. It was at this point that Flying Officer Edwards arrived on the scene. His orders were to back up the markers on the western aiming point, and that is exactly what he did; his bomb-aimer, Flying Officer Skingley, dropped a neat pattern of ten red spot fires precisely on target. As Cheshire had realised, the way the raid was developing, pin-point accuracy within the target area was no longer of the first importance. The depot by now, in Deane's dramatic phrase, was a "Technicolor inferno", and the main force bomb-aimers, looking down through their bomb-sights, would aim for what seemed to them to be the centre of the markers. Nevertheless, it was Cheshire's duty to get the marking right, and Edwards had his blessing.

The timing of the second marking, taking account of the difference between his H-hour and Cheshire's, would be confirmed by Deane at the Coningsby debriefing. He would continue: "Ordered in [the second wave to bomb] by RT and WT. From the many HF transmissions it was obvious that all had not received message so repeated continuously on HF from 0029 to 0033 hours. Reception on Channel 'C' very bad owing to British broadcast being on same frequency."

Somehow, between them, Deane and Sparks got their message through. Recrimination ceased, the radios were silent; the waiting 1 Group pilots turned towards the target. For many of their number, the message came too late: the yield of those dreadful seeds was fully grown.

When John Butcher of 626 Squadron, in UM K-King Two, reached the assembly-point, nine miles north-north-west of Mailly-le-Camp, he heard an RT message "Rat Two, wait". Taking this to come from the "Master of Ceremonies" (from his Berlin experience, he continued to think of whoever was in charge by that designation) he obediently commenced a rate-one left-hand orbit, centred on the bright yellow markers which were burning on the ground. After a few minutes, his mid-upper gunner, Flight Sergeant Joe Francis, a twenty-year old from Toronto, informed him that a number of Ju-88s were in the orbit, too, and that their presence was making it a most unhealthy place to be. Butcher, accordingly, flattened out his turn, extending the radius of King Two's orbit and, as he hoped, keeping at a distance from the danger area.

Flight Sergeant Carroll, arriving in PH B-Baker a few moments later, circled the assembly-point and listened out for orders. Hearing only an "American news broadcast", he asked his wireless operator if anything were coming through on the Marconi. There was something, Sergeant Lawrence reported, but so garbled was the message that he could not tell who was transmitting or to what purpose. Had Lawrence, at that moment, been attending to the "Fishpond" set instead of listening to the wireless, he might have had warning of the single-engined fighter which, at that moment, was closing on B-Baker. Sergeants Garlick in the mid-upper turret and Appleyard in the rear, however, were thoroughly alert ("twitching distinctly" was Garlick's expression): seeing a long stream of tracer almost dead astern, they called on Carroll to commence a corkscrew, and both fired short bursts of bullets - more to let the "bandit" know they had seen him than in any hope of hitting him, for he stayed out of their range. One minute later, they saw another stream of tracer, on the starboard quarter, and the same, or a similar, single-engined fighter. Carroll expended a few more ergs of energy in another corkscrew, and the fighter disappeared. "A hit-and-run merchant," was Garlick's scornful verdict, "and more run than hit." Within the next two hours, he was to have a worthier antagonist.

For the crew of 12 Squadron's PH Q-Queenie, it was also the assembly-point fracas which marked the nadir of the mission. The target was in sight, the attack had clearly started, and Maxwell was disappointed to hear the order "Wait". Like Butcher and Carroll, however, he commenced a left-hand orbit around the yellow spot fires, and quickly realised that he was hazarding his life. For one thing, the piece of sky he was flying in was heavily populated by a lot of other aircraft, many of whom were firing at each other; for another, one segment of his orbit coincided with a localised, but persistent, stream of heavy flak. At the height he was flying, there was no vital need for artificial oxygen, but there was a popular theory that it enhanced night-vision: he told Crighton to turn the valve to "High".

Another aircraft in the orbit was 12 Squadron's PH C-Charlie, flown by Pilot Officer Stewart Black of the RCAF. Following Carroll's aircraft down the

runway at Wickenby, Black had set out on the nineteenth operation of a tour
which had begun with consecutive sorties to Berlin on 27th and 28th January
1943 (coincidentally, the last two trips of your author's tour at Wickenby).
Black's rear gunner, Sergeant Dick Woodruff, at the age of thirty-two, was
several years older than the rest of his crew - older, indeed, than the majority of
aircrew, and he differed from many in that he had made his way in civil life
before the war began. He had gathered at the briefing that this was to be a quick
in-and-out trip to some woodland east of Paris where a Panzer division was
believed to be encamped. Since it was only to count as a third of an "op", since
all sorts of diversionary raids had been laid on to keep the Jerry fighters busy,
and particularly since a number of fairly senior officers were taking the
opportunity to get their bottoms off the ground, he had hopes that the attack on
Mailly-le-Camp, or whatever they called the place, would be a piece of cake.

It was the mêlée over the assembly-point that had changed Woodruff's
mind. Black had commenced to orbit in what Woodruff likened to a swarm of
gnats on a warm summer evening. From six to twelve thousand feet, the sky
above the yellow markers was thick with Lancasters and, at their scheduled
height of ten thousand, C-Charlie's crew were right in the middle of the
crowd. Woodruff, ceaselessly swinging his turret, fingers on the triggers, saw
the twin-engined Messerschmitts and Junkers flashing by, witnessed combat
after combat, and watched one Lancaster after another fall out of the sky.
Several times, he and the mid-upper gunner, Warrant Officer MacDonald,
fired bursts from their Brownings at the passing shadows but, so close
together were the bombers that, when a fighter fired its guns, they couldn't
tell whether C-Charlie was the target or the next one in the stream. A
Lancaster moved close enough for him to see, in the moonlight, the big,
painted letters "PH" - the 12 Squadron code - beside the roundel on its
fuselage, and he watched, horrified, as the aircraft was smashed into a mass
of burning, falling debris by a night-fighter's cannon-fire. It was after this
aerial shambles had continued for ten or twelve minutes that one of the pilots
finally lost his patience, and his self-control. Through the roar of the
slipstream, the growl of the engines and the rattle of gunfire, hundreds of
airmen heard his voice in their headphones and, in their hearts, they echoed
his appeal. "Come on, Master Bomber, pull your finger out!"

It seemed a mild enough remonstrance and, in the circumstances, not
unreasonable, but it broke all the rules of RT discipline - rules learned and
accepted, in training and in practice, throughout the Command for many years.
Even on intercom, between members of a crew, talk was kept to a minimum by
every airman with an interest in survival; no casual chatter, in case those first,

vital words from a gunner to his pilot "Fighter, fighter" failed to reach his ears. As for air-to-air traffic, that was strictly one-way only, and no talking back. In your author's experience of bomber operations, it had only happened once - on a bad night over Berlin, when a Master of Ceremonies had remarked, in what struck many as a patronising tone, "Come along in, Main Force, the searchlights won't bite you", and received the succinct riposte he deserved.

The trouble with indiscipline is that it tends to be infectious. It might have been halted if, at the start, an authoritative voice had been heard to make some prophylactic statement, perhaps "Hang on, chaps, the markers will be going down in a few minutes", but no-one spoke to that effect, nor yet to any other, until it was too late for many of their number. Then, the only word was "Wait!" The Lancasters went on circling, while pilots demanded that the Master Bomber, or Master of Ceremonies, should call them in to bomb. Some believed they were addressing Wing Commander Cheshire; few seemed to know, or to remember, that their recourse, albeit a forbidden one, was to the Main Force Controller, Wing Commander Deane, and he, could they have heard him, was telling them the same: "Do not bomb - wait!"

CHAPTER SIX

NIGHT FIGHTERS' PICNIC

Leonard Cheshire, although desperately worried by what he could see was happening over the assembly-point, could not hear the pleas for action, let alone reply to them. His RT was tuned to the frequency of his Mosquitos, of Wing Commander Deane and the flare-force Lancasters. Looking back later at his post-attack report, he made this further comment: "I notice it contains no reference to the effort I made to order the Main Force to break off the attack and return home. Exactly when during the attack I started issuing this order I cannot remember, but it was shortly after the furious air battle started. The combination of the attack going wrong with the sight of aircraft being shot down convinced me that it was my duty to order everybody back to base as soon as possible, for in my judgement the further damage the aircraft were likely to do to the target would not justify the large losses we were likely to suffer. In the whole of my operational career I had never seen so many aircraft going down in so short a space of time and I knew that this could only be because most of the available Luftwaffe night fighters were in the sky and with the bright moon our aircraft would have little chance. To this day I can remember my near despair at finding no way of getting through either to the Controller or directly to the aircraft themselves."

"Two of my crew are dead already," someone shouted, "for Christ's sake do something, or we're all going to die." Out of the flash-broken darkness came a dusty answer, delivered in a harsh, Australian twang: "Die like a man, then, you yellow bastard. And do it quietly." That may have raised a quiet, sardonic chuckle in a few bomber cabins, but it didn't stop the protests - or the reprimands.

"What the hell's happening," asked a plaintive voice, "where are the markers?"

"If this is a third of an op," growled another, in a Canadian accent, "I'm half-way to going LMF."

"Shut up," came a rebuke. "What are the Jerries going to think of the RAF, hearing all this?"

"F... you, and the RAF - I'm RCAF!"

"I don't mind dicing," argued one pilot, "but this is bloody suicide!"

Another pilot in that unhealthy orbit was Wing Commander Garner, the newly-appointed Commander of 166 Squadron, at the controls of Kirmington's AS C-Charlie. He was flying the first operation of his Service career. That an officer of his rank, in the General Duties branch (the flying branch), should have had no contact with the enemy in over four years of war may seem surprising, but it was not by any means unknown. There were those so efficient in filling their appointments - perhaps in a staff job, or in a training role - that their superiors refused to let them go; there were others who somehow got stuck in the system and couldn't disentangle themselves from the red tape; there were also a few who were prepared to deny themselves, for however long it took, both the thrill of being shot at and the chance of glory. The crew of C-Charlie were not as yet sure into which of these categories their new captain fell. It had, in fact, been something of a shock to discover that morning that their previous skipper, a second tour pilot who was also their flight commander, and with whom they had flown fifteen successful operations, had entirely gone from Kirmington, with no word of farewell, leaving his crew to the new squadron commander as a going concern.

From what Sergeant Louis Wayte, C-Charlie's rear gunner, could hear on the intercom, the delay in the action over Mailly-le-Camp was due to the pall of smoke and the dust, caused by earlier bombs, which was obscuring the aiming point, and that someone - whom he believed to be Cheshire - would shortly re-mark it, if they would all shut up and let him get on with it. Wayte saw a lot of combats in progress (many years later, when asked about his feelings, he gave an honest, Christian answer: "I prayed," he said, "that the enemy would not come nigh unto us"), but the aspect of the orbit which caused him most concern was that by no means all the pilots were making left-hand turns: he saw, from his turret, the exhaust flames of aircraft going past him in the opposite direction.

Still the bombers circled, and anxiety turned to anger. The unknown Master Bomber was reviled. Then another voice was heard, clipped and high-pitched, shaking with emotion: "This is a Wing Commander speaking. I order you to stop all transmissions on RT. Anyone who knows who the transgressors are is to report their identity on landing." Some seconds passed in silence after that.

In the rear turret of C-Charlie, Louis Wayte heard the voice he thought of as Cheshire's, but which in all probability that of Neville Sparks, saying "Rat Two, bomb. Come on, all you insolent bastards, everybody - bomb!" Wayte was pleased to note that, throughout the whole episode, his new captain had remained impassive.

The other 'sprog' 166 Squadron captain, Flying Officer Warmington, had been wondering if operations were normally like this. Even his outbound flight hadn't gone so well as planned, owing to a misunderstanding with the navigator about what speed he ought to fly. They had begun to realise that AS B-Baker's airspeed was too high when the DR position on the first leg over France had failed to match the fixes on the navigator's radar. Warmington had circled a dim light on the ground, unaware, in his innocence, that he was orbiting a night-fighter's holding point. A report from the mid-upper gunner that a twin-engined aircraft was also in the orbit had prompted him to find another way of losing time. Despite all his efforts, he had reached the assembly-point five minutes earlier than he had intended. He had heard the order "Wait" but, deciding that he had done enough orbiting already, had made a slow turn to the north and gained a thousand feet of altitude. After a few minutes, the angry voices had sounded in his headphones: "Let's bomb and get the hell out of here", "Finger, Master Bomber", and "Shut up, the Jerries will be laughing at us". The remarks had surprised him, because his teaching had been that all such chatter was utterly tabu. He had turned towards the target, away again and back again, for seventeen minutes, before the order came to bomb, and in that time he saw what he would later describe as "glows in the sky, pools of white and orange fire marking the ground below and lighting the scene like daylight - but they weren't markers, every one was a Lancaster."

Warmington's rear gunner, Andreas Moldt, in his later document, would tell what happened when B-Baker made its bombing run:

"Soon the cookies started exploding, and we could feel it at our height. The sky was lit by exploding bombs and fires on the ground. Behind us and a little lower was another Lanc, and behind him a twin-engined aircraft, and that could only be a fighter. I set my sight on it but found, when correcting for distance, that my line of sight was too close to the Lancaster. I tried to inform Ivon and ask him to lose a little height, but he and John were occupied getting us on a steady course to bomb seconds later, and there were all the noises - music and voices, more or less distorted - from the RT on the intercom making it impossible to communicate among the crew. The German fired and the Lanc was shot down. I have often wondered what I could have done to warn the pilot: I thought of firing, but that would only have distracted him. Then there was a terrific noise from all the bombs exploding within a few minutes. The aircraft was jumping and bouncing over the target. We were very close to other aircraft at times but a quick reaction from the skipper prevented a collision. There was a terrific explosion just before we bombed, most likely from the ammunition dump."

Events in the depot were as fearful and as bloody as over the assembly-point. Deafened by the succession of monstrous explosions, choked and blinded by the acrid smoke and dust, the Panzertruppen crouched in whatever shelter they could find and tried to stay alive until the nightmare ended. Outside the barracks, a system of zig-zag trenches, two metres deep, had been prepared for just such an emergency. They were adequate protection against flying splinters, but so great was the earthquake when a "cookie" exploded, even at some distance, that the sides crumbled in upon the men inside. The dilemma of the soldiers who were trapped was whether to fight their way to the surface - if they had the strength - and risk the flying fragments, or to stay where they were and hope that someone eventually would come and dig them out. After what seemed like a lifetime, although the roar of the bombers still filled the night, the intensity of bombing suddenly decreased. The shouts of NCOs were heard in the darkness: "All soldiers not in possession of their weapons, ammunition and field-kit, go and get them now. The rest of you - fight the fires. Move!" Some men could not move, some did not care to, and

Aiming point photograph, 166 Sqn. (Andreas Molt)

some would never move again. Others, however, hurried to obey, and found that they were caught in the open by a yet more dreadful onslaught.

In 12 Squadron's PH Q-Queenie, ignoring all distractions, Maxwell had flown orbits for a long twenty minutes, losing count of how often, and of how many Lancasters he had seen go down in flames. He had expected to receive the order to bomb from what he thought of as a flying Operations Room, but that never happened. The word came at last from someone who called himself the Deputy Controller and who, as we know, was Squadron Leader Sparks: "Rat Two, bomb". By that time, Maxwell didn't care who gave the order: it could have been Tommy Handley or Wynford Vaughan Thomas, so long as he gave it. Gratefully, he swung Q-Queenie's nose towards the target; some

hundred and fifty other pilots did the same. Maxwell's situation resembled that
of a jockey when the starting gate goes up at Aintree, or of a bargain-hunter
when the doors of Harrod's open for the Autumn sales. Conscious of
Lancasters close above, below and on either side of him, with Q-Queenie
bouncing in their slipstream, Maxwell concentrated on following his bomb-
aimer's directions as promptly and smoothly as he could.

Paddy O'Hara, lying prone in the nose, oblivious of other aircraft and the
long, bright streams of tracer that were hosing around him, keeping the target-
marker in the cross-wires of his bomb-sight, flicked on his microphone.
"Steady...steady...left...left a touch, Skipper, that's it, and steady...steady..."

Maxwell felt the Lancaster lift as the four-ton bomb-load fell; O'Hara
craned forward and, looking down through the perspex, watched the
enormous, cylinder-shaped "cookie" and the cluster of five-hundred pounders
as they dropped in formation, silhouetted against the lurid scene below.
"Bombs gone!" he shouted.

Maxwell reached down and pulled up the lever. "Bomb-doors closed," he
responded, and opened the throttles. "Let's get the hell out of here." It was his
practice, as it was your author's, by tipping the wings alternately at frequent
intervals, to give his gunners a view of what, in level flight, was their blind
spot - underneath the fuselage. As he levelled out from the manoeuvre, Q-
Queenie shuddered, as though at some offence. For a moment, Maxwell
thought he might have touched wings with another aircraft, then he saw
tongues of flame flickering back from both port engines, and knew he had
been hit. Simultaneously, he heard Jim Davidson's voice, clear and urgent in
his headphones: "Pilot from mid-upper, the port wing's on fire."

Maxwell pulled back the left-hand throttles, turned the rudder-trim to
starboard to counteract the drag, and told Jack Crighton to cut off the fuel
supply to the port engines; together they pressed the buttons to feather the
propellers, and energised the fire-extinguishers. He watched the engines
closely, and saw the flames continue, enveloping the entire inboard section of
the wing. The port-outer propeller was windmilling. "Try feathering it again,"
he told Crighton.

"No good, Skipper, the electrics have gone. I reckon it's a case of jump
or roast."

"Often, in his dreams, Maxwell had visualised this moment, while never
believing that it would really come. It was a moment that every pilot dreads.
"Crew from Captain," he said into his microphone, "abandon aircraft. I repeat,
abandon aircraft."

Within seconds, Crighton had clipped a parachute-pack to the pilot's harness, and ducked under the instrument-panel into the nose. There, O'Hara released the escape-hatch door and dropped it overboard. He waited for Crighton to go out through the hatch, followed by Lloyd, and then dropped out himself. On his way through the cabin, Maurice Garlick paused beside Maxwell and shouted in his ear. "We're just south of the target. Walk south-eastwards when you're down." The pilot, struggling to hold Q-Queenie straight and level, nodded, and Garlick disappeared into the nose. Watching the burning wing carefully (if it broke in two, and the aircraft fell into a spin, the odds would be against him when he tried to jump), Maxwell called each crew station in turn. Receiving no answer, he knew his job was done. With the fingers of his right hand, he felt for the release-grip of the pack clipped on his chest and, for a few unpleasant seconds, failed to find it. Then he realised what had happened: Crighton had attached the pack the wrong way round. Briefly, Maxwell wondered whether he should unclasp and re-attach it, decided he could pull as well with his left hand as his right, and followed his crew into the outer darkness.

There was a strange fiction, conceived in 1943, which was given credence by most bomber crews, including your author's, throughout the rest of the war and for many years afterwards, that the shot and shell discharged at them occasionally included a piece of pyrotechnic wizardry known as a scarecrow flare. This device, on exploding, produced a close resemblance to an aircraft being hit with all its bombs on board, and was intended, so the story went, to inspire such alarm and despondency among the bomber men as would put them off their aim. Technically, the stratagem was possible, if of formidable proportions; practically, it made no sense at all. If the heavy anti-aircraft guns could fire missiles full of fireworks close enough to a Lancaster or a Halifax to frighten the crew out of their wits, it would surely have occurred to the efficient Luftwaffe flak troops that they would be better employed firing 8.8 centimetre shells which, with a lethal range of thirty yards, could knock them out of the sky.

Post-war research into German records has produced no evidence that scarecrow flares were ever deployed or that they even existed. The probability is that the awesome, multi-coloured, billowing phenomena were caused by real bombers, full of high explosive, incendiaries, petrol and oxygen, and possibly of marker flares, either colliding with each other or receiving a direct hit in the bomb-bay, and that some psychologist, professional or amateur, within the world of RAF Intelligence, decided that it would be better for morale if the aircrews believed them to be no more than the product of a cunning German hoax.

The attack as seen from a distance of 15kms, by an amateur photographer in the village of Fresnay.

Several instances of the phenomena were reported by crews over Mailly-le-Camp. In 166 Squadron's AS B-Baker, Flying Officer Warmington's crew had successfully delivered their first ever bomb-load, the photo had been taken, and the bomb-doors closed. "We had just settled down," Warmington would remember, "on the heading into the comfort of the jet-black darkness, when the whole sky lit up, with red, green and white streaks in all directions, like a massive star with thousands of points, hanging in the sky until a couple of minutes later, when we passed through the same airspace and all was dark again." Warmington, as a "sprog" captain, had not yet been indoctrinated with the "scarecrow" theory, and he made his own assessment of what he had seen: "It could only have been a Lancaster Pathfinder exploding with all its load of target markers." (That judgement, however, was not entirely accurate. The explosion Warmington saw may well have been caused by a Lancaster, but not by a Pathfinder: none was hit with its cargo on board.)

Unlike Warmington and most 1 Group pilots, Stewart Black in 12 Squadron's PH C-Charlie had only made one orbit - albeit a wide one - before he heard the message "All clear to bomb", but eight minutes had been long enough for both him and his rear gunner, Sergeant Woodruff, to be convinced, not only of the shambles among the bomber force, but that many scarecrow flares were exploding all around them. Indeed, just after the bombs had gone, at 0029 hours, Woodruff's composure was shaken by what he took to be a big one, which detonated so close to C-Charlie that pieces of its structure, rolling off his turret-top, seemed to cling to the barrels of his guns for several eerie seconds before sinking down past his clear-vision panel. Black, however, knew that this explosion was no hoax: he knew that it was caused by a stricken Lancaster flying alongside him which, in its death-throes, had skidded into C-Charlie, colliding with the bomb-doors, fracturing an oil-pipe and damaging the starboard-outer engine. Maintaining an altitude of 8,000 feet, he flew back at the best speed he could make on the three remaining engines and, half way home over France, was comforted to find that he had an escort of two sister Lancasters - one on each wing. Standing in the astro-dome, Warrant Officer Roy Holding, the navigator, tried to read their code-letters, but they were just too far away. "I don't know what squadron those guys are from," he remarked, "but they're our guardian angels tonight".

Flight Lieutenant Breckenridge, in 626 Squadron's UM X-ray Two, had survived the waiting time over the assembly-point, where the experience of Biff Baker, a second-tour man, in the mid-upper turret, had helped him to avoid both the dangers of collision and the attentions of the fighters. X-ray Two's bombs went down at twenty-nine minutes after midnight - at the same

time as C-Charlie's and just two minutes after the attack should have ended.
The bomb-aimer, Flying Officer Poushinsky (another Canadian) saw his four-
thousand pounder hit a building immediately to the west of the spot fire he was
aiming at, but he was never going to have a photograph to prove it. Before the
photo-flash exploded, and despite his anguished appeal for half a minute's
level flight, his pilot followed Baker's advice to "Get weaving, skipper, and
don't stop until we're over Wickenby."

Sixty seconds behind Black and Breckenridge, John Butcher made his
bombing run in UM K-King Two at 7,000 feet. Looking through the bomb-
sight, George Wilson saw the neat rows of buildings outlined by the markers
and the flashes of the bombs. To Sergeant Joe Francis, in the rear turret, it
seemed that the aircraft was bouncing and jolting like a truck on a pot-holed
country road, and he realised that the bounces were caused by shock waves
from the cookies exploding in the depot. You never noticed those shock
waves, he thought, from 20,000 feet.

Many a Bomber Command air gunner completed his tour without firing a
single shot in anger; many another never saw a fighter. Some saw the fighter,
fought and lost the battle; some saw nothing before they were destroyed. Others
were in combat and lived to tell the story; those who fought and won were in a
minority. On that May night in 1944, there were confrontations of all kinds in
the skies of northern France, on the approach to the target, on the bombing run
and on the journey home. In many cases, it was the night-fighters who won.

Among the crews who barely glimpsed their destroyer was that of the
"Elint" Halifax, DT V-Victor. They had been in the target area since the first
TIs went down, had heard the hiatus over the RT, and had seen, below them,
the Lancasters falling like fiery boulders in a hellish avalanche. When all
activity had ceased above the depot, and Harry Gibson had decided that his
work was done, V-Victor's position was some twenty miles south-east of
Mailly-le-Camp. The flight engineer, John Ackroyd, aged twenty-one, from
Dewsbury in Yorkshire, began to calculate V-Victor's fuel requirements for the
journey home. Many years later, he recalled what happened next:

"It was nearly 0100 hours when suddenly a fighter - I think
it was an Me-109 - loomed up and opened fire. It all happened so
quick. The port inner engine was ablaze, and so was the root of
the main-plane - as if an acetylene burner was at work to cut it
off. I feathered the port inner and used the fire-extinguisher, but
it was no use. The intercom wasn't working, so I went to the rear
of the aircraft to tell the rest of the crew to bale out. The mid-

under gunner was dead. I went back to help the pilot. I fixed his parachute harness, which had come loose. I think the navigator, his assistant and the wireless op baled out through the front hatch, while the rest went out of the rear exit. This left Harry and myself. I followed him out with not much time to spare. We were under 5,000 feet. As I was going down, I saw the aircraft crash and blow up."

The bombers, however, had some notable successes, one of which was claimed by 1st Lieutenant Dawley's gunners, Sergeants Stephens and Percival, of the erstwhile jinx crew in 12 Squadron's PH V-Victor. They had arrived at the assembly-point at 8,000 feet, more or less on time, and had at first been amused to hear the AFN broadcast over the RT but, after ten minutes, when the news had ended and a dance band was playing "Deep in the heart of Texas", Dawley had tried another channel and heard, in stark contrast, the calm, last statement of the SD Flight leader: "I am hit and going down."

Dawley's bomb-aimer, Flight Sergeant Allen, the twenty-year old Yorkshireman who had been the chief disrupter of good order and discipline in the crew's days at Lindholme, described what happened next:

Sergeant Ackroyd, Flight Engineer in a Halifax of 192 Sqn's DT-V

"The instructions were to circle the flares until specifically ordered to bomb by the Master Bomber. There was a lot of chatter over the RT and evidence of planes being shot down. Dawley used his discretion, and started the bombing run. I spotted a FW-190 at three hundred yards port down. Dawley took corkscrew action and our gunners opened fire. We were hit in the port main-plane and undercarriage fairing. One of the fuel tanks was holed by an incendiary bullet, but it didn't explode. We found the shell afterwards in the engine nacelle. I think it was our rear gunner who scored the hit on the fighter. I saw it close in, on fire, on the starboard beam, and I thought for a moment that the pilot was going to ram us deliberately, and take us down with him. Then it turned over and dived into the ground."

In the course of the combat, V-Victor had veered away from the target and lost 2,000 feet of altitude. Allen called "dummy run" and the crew groaned in unison. Next time around, their only opposition came from the depot's remaining light flak guns. Mike Allen continued:

> "It appeared to be broad daylight. I don't recall if I aimed at the red spot fires or at the barrack buildings, which were clearly visible. I have no doubt I hit the target, although the photo didn't show it, probably because Dawley took violent evasive action immediately after bomb release, and the camera was badly angled. The rear gunner reported a sizeable explosion, with a lot of blue flashes, which may have indicated a hit on the power lines. Needless to say, Dawley scrubbed the low-level strafing…"

Another success, claimed by the gunners of 12 Squadron's PH F-Fox, was all the more notable because Flight Sergeant Dyer-Matthews and his crew were engaged in the first operation of their tour. Apart from the navigator, Flying Officer Jack Brownhill from Ontario, all the crew were NCOs, and all, understandably, had been feeling rather nervous. They had flown the orbits as ordered (and heard a lot of chatter over the RT, which instructors at their training schools had told them shouldn't happen), bombed when they were told to and started out for home. Five minutes later, at 8,000 feet above the River Aube, Sergeant Derbyshire, in the rear turret, noticed an aircraft high on the port quarter, some 800 yards away, moving towards him in a diving turn. He switched on his microphone and rapped out "Fighter, fighter, prepare to corkscrew port," in the way he had been taught and had practised with his pilot at the HCU. He thought it was a fighter, because it only had two engines and hadn't the appearance of a PFF Mosquito, and his opinion was confirmed when, at 600 yards, its guns began to fire. Then he shouted "Corkscrew port, go!" and opened fire himself. He fired four hundred rounds, a hundred from each gun, and Sergeant Butler joined in with a burst from the mid-upper turret. At three hundred yards, Derbyshire was sure his bullets had struck home: burning and spinning, the fighter vanished from his sight. "Okay, skipper," he said, "you can resume course. I think I got it."

"Good show," said Dyer-Matthews, and checked his instruments. He was surprised to discover that, during the corkscrew, F-Fox had lost 1,500 feet of altitude and was ninety degrees off course. That wasn't quite the way he had been taught to fly a standard corkscrew.

626 Squadron's UM E-Easy Two, at 8,000 feet above the assembly-point, was attacked by an unidentified twin-engined aircraft, diving in from the

starboard quarter high. Flight Sergeant Bladon's mid-upper gunner, Sergeant Lowe, ordered "Corkscrew starboard", and fired a five-second burst, at which the fighter broke away and disappeared.

Another twin-engined night-fighter attacked AS K-King of 166 Squadron, twenty minutes after Flight Sergeant Gibson, RNZAF, and his crew had left the target and were nearing Fontainebleau on the first homeward leg. In the ensuing combat, the Lancaster was damaged, losing an engine, but the fighter was destroyed. So much fuel had been expended in the desperate battle, during which the throttles had been set at combat power, that the gauges were reading zero when K-King reached the Sussex coast. Gibson flew directly to the 11 Group fighter airfield at Tangmere, ten miles north of Selsey Bill; the three remaining engines cut on the approach, but he had sufficient skill - and airspeed in hand - to make a "dead-stick" landing.

A few minutes after Flight Sergeant Gibson's combat, 1st Lieutenant Dawley's PH V-Victor, flying at 9,000 feet on the homeward track, south-west of Fontainebleau, received a second attack from a single-engined fighter. This one - a Messerschmitt Bf-109 - was spotted by Sergeant Percival, the rear gunner, astern of and below him at 400 yards range. Dawley, on instruction, made a diving turn to port, and Ted Percival fired four hundred rounds, at which the fighter broke away on the starboard beam, and did not reappear.

Flight Sergeant Carroll of 12 Squadron, flying homeward in PH B-Baker, was at 15,000 feet above the hills west of Chartres when, at ten minutes past two in the morning, he heard the call "Corkscrew" for the third time on the mission. There had been no "Fishpond" warning, but his gunners, Garlick and Appleyard, had reacted on seeing the tracer streaming at them, and their call came just in time: the first salvo from the night-fighter narrowly missed them as Carroll threw B-Baker into a diving turn to port. When the gunners saw the night-fighter, at four hundred yards astern, they both opened fire, and it broke off the attack, only to re-position high on the port quarter and come diving in again. As Carroll pulled the nose up for a climbing turn towards it, a long, raking burst hit B-Baker in the starboard fin and elevator, and in the starboard wing. The rear-turret guns stopped firing, and Garlick feared that Appleyard was hit (the gunner told him later that all four guns had jammed); then the black shape of the fighter filled his gun-sight, and he saw his tracer strike its fuselage and port engine. "The bandit's breaking away, skipper," said Garlick. "Maintain your turn for a minute so I can watch him. His port engine's on fire - he's going down."

As the fighter hit the ground in a vivid burst of flame, Garlick's heart rejoiced: not for the fact that he had killed those German airman, but because he knew that, by his action, he had saved B-Baker and the lives of all her crew. They shared his elation: even Bill Lawrence, the wireless operator, whose favourite pastime was punching Garlick's nose, admitted that the sound of the mid-upper guns had been like music to his ears (an emotion which, sadly, did not survive his first two pints of beer on the next crew outing). Back home at Wickenby, both the gunners were slightly shaken when they saw the row of bullet-holes which ran diagonally along B-Baker's fuselage from the top of the rear turret to the base of the mid-upper. Garlick claimed an He-111 as destroyed. It was only after more mature reflection, and having checked the silhouettes in the Gunnery Section, that he realised he should have claimed a Bf-110.

Five thousand feet above the English Channel, at half-past two in the morning, Pilot Officer Ayres of 626 Squadron pressed button "A" on his RT set and made the promised, discreet call: "Sugar Two from Mike Two, are you receiving me, over?" Hearing nothing but a whisper of static in his headphones, he tried again. There was still no reply, and there never would be. Norman Fisher's crew, on their first operation, had flown fifty miles of the homeward route and were nearing Fontainebleau when a night-fighter caught them and shot them down in flames. UM S-Sugar Two crashed at Montigny le Guesdier, in the province of Seine-et-Marne, and all the crew died instantly. They are buried side by side in the commune's small cemetery.

EM F-Fox of 207 Squadron was hit in the starboard wing by cannon shells from a night-fighter over the target. The shells destroyed the panel covering the dinghy, which promptly inflated and was thrown back above the tail-plane like an enormous hoop-la ring. A second attack caused a fire in the bomb-bay, and a third was sufficient to destroy the Lancaster. Five of the crew made their escape by parachute, but Warrant Officer Lissette of the RNZAF was still at the controls when F-Fox hit the ground seven miles south-east of Namours in Seine-et-Marne.

Among the crews who were neither fired upon nor fired at a fighter was that of Flight Sergeant Smith, in 626 Squadron's UM Y-Yoke Two. They were nearing the half-way point of their tour (their latest operation had been their thirteenth, and everyone was glad when that was over). The crew's rear gunner, Sergeant Gallagher, had left his home in County Cork in the early days of 1939 with the object of enlisting in the RAF. At that time, his services had been peremptorily declined but, when the war began, the RAF had changed its mind. "Keen on flying?" he had been asked. "We've got just the job for you." The nearest he had come to aviation for the next three years had been at the ground end of a barrage balloon's cable. "Green as a cabbage, I was," he was later to admit. "It took me three years to get into aircrew." Of Mailly-le-Camp, he remembered this: "At the briefing, great emphasis was put on accurate bombing. I had a chuckle with the bomb-aimer about disturbing the slumbers of the German troops. I felt confident because I expected an easy target, but I was a bit apprehensive about the moonlight. Communications over the target were poor, and I got the impression that the Master Bomber had been shot down. There was a lot of chatter, and I heard a pilot call for silence to give his gunners a chance. I focused my attention on our tail more intensely than ever - I was ultra-vigilant. The most reassuring thing I heard was the cultured English public school accent of a pilot asking 'I say, which field are we supposed to bomb?' I hope he survived the war. On the return journey, we were trailed as far as the French coast, but we weren't attacked. We must have been extremely lucky to return unharmed."

Flying Officer Furlong's crew, in 103 Squadron's PM V-Victor, were among those who survived direct attack. Mailly-le-Camp was their third operation which, under the new edict, would give them an aggregate of exactly one. Considering the arithmetic, the reargunner, Sergeant John Norman, a twenty-two year old erstwhile shop-assistant from Cambridge, felt a touch of gloom: "I came to the conclusion that we should all be dead before the end." He was determined, however, that if they had to die, it would be through no fault of his, nor of his armament. As for that, he had some misgivings about the effect of the incendiary rounds in his ammunition: "I was never an enthusiast of tracer," he was later to admit. "In practice at night, I could never see the drogue once I had opened fire, and on ops it was an absolute give-away. I wonder how many bombers were lost through giving their position away by a burst of fire." In this, he was expressing a view shared by several battle-hardened gunners and, furthermore, by some night-fighter pilots, at least one of whom - the German Emil Nonnenmacher - insisted on his forward-firing guns being armed with non-tracer bullets. Over Mailly-le-Camp, however, Norman had no cause to fire any kind of bullet: he never saw the Bf-110 which came from dead ahead - only the tracer as it passed above his turret. Nor did the mid-upper gunner have time to fire, so quickly did the fighter appear and disappear.

John Norman's story, as he told it later, provided yet another instance of the "scarecrow flare" myth. He had reported seeing several of them over the target, and later, when J-Jig eventually returned to Elsham Wolds (having been diverted to Kirmington at first), the flight engineer was derisive: "Scarecrows, my foot. Explosions, bits of wing and fuselage burning and falling - that's what I saw."

In PM U-Uncle, another 103 Squadron aircraft, Flight Sergeant Brownings' crew were nearing the halfway point of their tour, and living on what many would regard as borrowed time, for they had been attacked by fighters on every one of their first ten missions. On the fourth, towards the end of the Battle of Berlin, the rear gunner, Sergeant Bob Thomas, had died in his turret while fighting off the first of three attacks from a Focke-Wulf 190, and it had taken all Fred Brownings' strength and skill to fly the crippled aircraft home. Now, approaching Mailly-le-Camp on his fourteenth operation, he heard the RT instruction to orbit the assembly-point.

The wireless operator, twenty-one year old Flight Sergeant Spark from Carlisle, was later to describe what happened next. "The skipper told us to keep our eyes skinned, as he was going to make a wide orbit well away from the yellow markers. I took up my position in the astro-dome and watched the port quarter and beam for night-fighters. Each member of the crew had a piece of sky to watch and we religiously stuck to it. We had learned the hard way, and we knew that survival depended on seeing the enemy first. During the ten minutes or so we were orbiting, I saw three Lancasters attacked and shot down. It was absolute chaos on the RT, with crews cursing the Master Bomber, and an American news broadcast coming over on the same frequency. After what seemed hours we heard a voice through the mush on the RT saying 'Go in and bomb'. Needless to say, we didn't waste any time. As we were leaving the target, the rear gunner, Sergeant Burrell, spotted a FW-190 coming in from dead astern and yelled 'Corkscrew starboard, go!' He fired one long burst at us, but missed, and thankfully we lost him after that."

Flying Officer Parmenter's crew, in 166 Squadron's AS J-Jig Two, were at the beginning of their tour, and Sergeant Swaffield, a twenty-two year-old apprentice motor mechanic from Crewkerne in Somerset, who had already completed nine operations, including the bad one to Nuremberg and several to the Ruhr, was not entirely delighted to find himself among them, deputising for a

Jack Spark, DFM Wireless Operator on 103 Sqn's PM-U.

sick flight engineer. Bill Swaffield had made little of the disjointed chatter over the RT, and had failed to understand why his temporary skipper had flown around in circles for a long twenty minutes before going in to bomb. Like John Norman, he had accepted, after Nuremberg, that he would not survive a tour, but he didn't want to die with someone else's crew while his own were sleeping soundly in their beds. His heart had lifted when the bombs went down, only to fall when they were attacked by night-fighters twice in succession. The pilot, however took the right evasive action and the gunners blazed away at every opportunity. Nobody was hurt, nothing was damaged; Flying Officer Parmenter flew J-Jig Two, and a grateful Sergeant Swaffield, away from where the trouble was and safely home to Kirmington.

There were many more combats, of which the crews would tell when they landed at their bases early in the morning of Thursday, 4th May; there were other combats which could only be imagined, and other crews for whom there was to be no Thursday morning. In nine 1 Group squadrons, and in ten of 5 Group's, there would be names missing from the next battle order and the worst news of all to be wired to next of kin.

Pilot Officer Norman Barker, DFC, of Toronto, bomb aimer of Fred Browning's crew in 103 Sqn's PM-U.

CHAPTER SEVEN

THE FINAL MOMENTS

In the account he was to write thirty years later, Laurence Deane described the final moments of the raid. Again, his recollection of the timing was, excusably, at fault. In this paragraph, taking "zero" to be one minute after midnight, between fifteen and twenty minutes should probably be added to the times he quotes.

"It was not until zero plus eighteen, when the concentration of bombing aircraft thinned out, that I became fully conscious of the field day the German night fighters were having. The vivid flashes of bombs bursting had been replaced by the flash of exploding Lancasters as they hit the ground - crashes we could literally hear and feel as well as see at our low altitude. By zero plus twenty all bombing activity had ceased. My deputy Neville Sparks called me over the RT and we agreed to head for home. The 'whoomff' we could feel and

hear as the Lancasters crashed continued: the night fighters
were still taking heavy toll. And tail-enders, of which I was
now one, were the easiest of prey for them. I used to enjoy my
after-raid eggs and bacon and I didn't want to be deprived
tonight. I therefore decided to deviate from the route laid down
for our return, which the night fighters were now patrolling,
and get down to zero feet. The crew took stations to look out
for pylons, chimneys etc., and we headed south along the route
we had selected, just north of Paris and on to Normandy. Low
flying is always exhilarating, and in the bright moonlight that
night it seemed to have a special kick - through outwitting the
Germans."

Those are the words of a seasoned campaigner - a veteran of many
Pathfinder missions.

Andreas Moldt, the Danish ex-seaman flying as Sergeant Petersen in 166
Squadron's AS B-Baker, on the other hand, had just embarked on his tour as
an air gunner. Later, he described the homeward flight:

"It was a nice feeling to know that we had crossed the
English coast. As we were still flying at 6,000 feet, oxygen
was not necessary, so I took off the mask and took hold of the
thermos flask of coffee, the barley sugar tablets and sultanas.
A cigarette would have been nice but that was strictly
prohibited. It was at this time that one started thinking back of
what had happened during the past hours. Even though it is
difficult to see an Englishman shaken, knowing them as well
as I did by now, I could sense that they were as shaken as I
was. There was very little talk on the intercom until we were
approaching base and the skipper and bomb-aimer were
looking for the airfield beacon flashing 'KM' in Morse code.
The squadron of butterflies that had been doing aerobatics in
my stomach for the last few hours finally landed and left me in
peace. One thing was clear to us now: if we were to get
through our tour it would only be through co-operation, mutual
respect and confidence.

We come into the circuit, the skipper makes a soft landing
and we roll to our dispersal where the ground crew are
waiting. The aircraft is inspected for damage - light flak
mostly had exploded around us - and the ground crew listen to
the engines before they are stopped. They have not been

damaged and are running as they should. It is a relief to get out of the flying gear. It is getting light as we board the crew bus, stow away our flying clothing and walk to the operations room for de-briefing. The intelligence and other specialists fill out a report for each crew. The more experienced crews say that it will take some time to find out what went wrong tonight. The Group Captain and the Wing Commander are there, the latter having taken part in the raid. The first thing one looks at when entering the room is a large blackboard listing the aircraft and their letters. When the captains arrive they write their names alongside their aircraft. It was easy to see who had not returned. Tonight, there are three - U-Uncle, E-Easy and Z-Zebra. One went down east-south-east of Paris, quite some distance off track, probably in combat with a fighter; one near Chartres, most likely hit by flak, and one near L'Aigle, also off track. The best part of the homecoming was a mug of tea with rum and then a cigarette, which we enjoyed before it was our turn to be de-briefed.

Our skipper was called aside by the Group Captain and asked what he thought about the night's events. Ivon said 'It's not for me to comment, Sir, this was my first operation, and I'm very pleased to be safely back at Kirmington.' The Group Captain said 'Quite so. Well done, Warmington.' He looked worried as he walked away. When de-briefing was finished we went to the Mess and had a good meal. A beer was allowed, but the wartime beer in England was not very strong. Alcohol was not forbidden, but we were advised not to use it - it could reduce one's night vision and that was a very important factor for us if we were to have a long and happy life.

We had been at Kirmington now for a week and during this time six crews and aircraft had been lost."

Of the thirty crews who had set out from Wickenby, at least twenty-one had dropped their bombs on the target; two more had aborted, and of the other seven the Squadron Adjutants would write in the Operations Record Books - "A/C failed to return, nothing heard after take-off". All that was known, for example, of Pilot Officer Carter's crew in 12 Squadron's PH H-Howe was that the aircraft hit the ground twenty-five miles east of Paris on the journey home; the only news of Flying Officer Ormrod's crew in PH Z-Zebra, Flight Sergeant Payne's in PH D-Dog, Flight Sergeant Barkway's in 626 Squadron's UM D-

Dog Two and of Pilot Officer Jackson's in UM Z-Zebra Two, was that they went down within a twelve-mile radius of Mailly-le-Camp, and that their physical remains were spread across the Champagne countryside between Nuisement-sur-Coole to the north of the target and St. Remy-sous-Barbuise to the south. (When he first joined the Squadron, Jackson had flown with your author on a mission to Berlin. My over-riding feeling, probably erroneous and certainly unprofitable, on learning of his end, was of responsibility - that I had somehow failed him on that "second-dickey trip").

Among those who made a safe return to Wickenby was 12 Squadron's PH V-Victor, with 1st Lieutenant Dawley at the wheel. Despite the self-sealing compound, petrol had spewed out of the punctured tank all the way from France, and it might have been prudent to land in southern England, but Dawley had a reason for getting back to base - a reason more cogent than the bacon and eggs that would be waiting in the Mess. His wife, back in Michigan, was expecting a baby, and he didn't want to be languishing at Manston or Woodbridge, waiting for repairs, when the good news came to Wickenby. He landed V-Victor there at twenty-four minutes after three in the morning of the fourth of May, and hurried to the operations building for de-briefing. The cable had arrived: he was the father of a daughter. Later that day, on V-Victor's nose, the ground crew artist painted a picture of a stork in flight, carrying a bomb wrapped in a nappy (or, in Dawley's terms, a diaper). Of his crew's work that night, the Gunnery Leader would write in the Squadron Combat Report: "Thorough sky search, and the quiet efficiency of both gunners, resulted in another fighter being downed. A claim of one FW-190 is made." With Peter Maxwell's crew delayed somewhere in France, Dawley and his men were indisputably the second squadron crew next to Black's in seniority, and the jinx was truly laid.

At Ludford Magna, 101 Squadron had despatched twenty aircraft, one of which returned early, because the mid-upper gunner had collapsed in his turret while the aircraft was still climbing over base. It was probably a 101 aircraft, flown by Pilot Officer Forsyth of the RNZAF, whose TOT was logged at nineteen minutes to one in the morning of 4th May, which was the last to bomb the target, but that cannot be stated as a fact: others may have followed whose TOTs were not recorded as they did not return. Of the remainder, the squadron lost four: SR Z-Zebra, flown by Flight Lieutenant Keard, was shot down near Aubeterre, eighteen miles south of the target, and the remains of Warrant Officer Drews' SR A-Apple were found near Dravegny, some sixty miles north-west of Mailly-le-Camp. One crew member from each of these two aircraft survived as a prisoner-of-war. SR X-ray Two crashed three miles north-east of the target, probably while Pilot Officer Baker was commencing his bombing run, and there were no survivors.

The fourth missing aircraft from 101 Squadron was SR J-Jig, piloted by Flying Officer Kenneth Muir. J-Jig's navigator was Flight Sergeant Nigel Lacey-Johnson, twenty-three years old, a native of Birmingham, who had been trained in South Africa under the Empire Flying Training Scheme in 1942, returning to England for the succession of courses which always preceded a posting to a squadron. At OTU, on Wellingtons, he had "crewed-up" with Sergeant Pilot Bowditch, a bomb-aimer, a wireless-operator and an air gunner. After completing the HCU course on Stirlings at Waterbeach, where the crew had grown to seven with the acquisition of a flight engineer and a second gunner, they had been posted to Wickenby to join 626 Squadron. On 24 February 1944, their pilot had been detailed, as was usual, to fly as "second-dickey" with a seasoned captain before he took the left-hand seat himself. The target was Schweinfurt; Bowditch's mentor was a veteran Australian, Flying Officer Hutchinson, whose tour had included a number of combats, an exemplary ditching, the long trips to Berlin and all points east. (Your author and his crew, "resting" between tours, were thoroughly inured to the fact that the best of fliers, and the best of comrades, were liable to die; they had nevertheless been shocked by the news that "Hutch" had gone down on his thirtieth and last.)

The headless crew had been packed off back to an HCU to find another pilot. When Flying Officer Muir had come along, they had been posted to Ludford Magna to join 101 Squadron and to acquire an eighth crew member - the German-speaking Pilot Officer Gorman who was to be their special operator on "Airborne Cigar". Mailly-le-Camp was their first operation - and their last. It can be assumed that they found and bombed the target, for the debris of J-Jig was scattered over the countryside some ten miles north of Troyes, on the first homeward leg. The bodies of the crew, recovered by the people of Voué, were buried that same night in the village churchyard, and the graves were marked with rough wooden crosses.

Between them, Nos. 103 and 576 Squadrons at Elsham Wolds had committed thirty-two aircraft - fourteen from 103 and eighteen from 576. Three of 103's and one of 576's failed to return. PM B-Baker, piloted by a 103 Squadron flight commander, Squadron Leader Swanston, and PM I-Ink, flown by Pilot Officer Rowe of the RAAF, were shot down in the orbit over the assembly-point; B-Baker crashed five miles to the west of Châlons-sur-Marne and I-Ink near the gaol-house in the town. Pilot Officer Holden's PM J-Jig went down north-east of Provins on the homeward route. There were no survivors from any of these aircraft. Among the more fortunate were the crew of PM U-Uncle, and Flight Sergeant Spark, the wireless-operator, later told of his return to Elsham Wolds: "There was considerable agitation at de-briefing, with all the crews complaining of the wait before receiving the order to bomb, and of the chaos caused by crews calling up on the same frequency. The Squadron lost twenty-one aircrew that night. Mailly-le-Camp had turned out to be a mini-Nuremberg."

It is probable that the missing 576 Squadron aircraft, UL B-Baker Two, flown by Pilot Officer Whalley, DFC, was shot down in the orbit, for it crashed north-west of Châlons-sur-Marne. Two of the crew survived and were taken prisoner. UL S-Sugar Two, with Pilot Officer Reed at the controls, was heavily damaged by a night-fighter, and returned to Elsham Wolds with a dead rear gunner and another crewman missing.

166 Squadron at Kirmington, despatching twenty-four aircraft, made a greater contribution to the force engaged in the attack than any other squadron. Twenty-one crews bombed the target, and three were shot down. AS E-Easy crashed seven miles east of Châlons-sur-Marne, probably after a running battle with a night-fighter which took Pilot Officer Myers and his crew a long way from their orbit of the assembly-point. From AS U-Uncle, which went down nine miles south of the target, Flight Sergeant Sanderson, RNZAF, and four members of his crew escaped by parachute, as did all but one of Pilot Officer Harrison's crew in AS Z-Zebra, when they were shot down twelve miles north-east of Sens.

When Z-Zebra's navigator, Sergeant Watson, returned to England with the help of the Resistance, he gave this account:

"We bombed from 6,000 feet at about 0030 hours, and set course on the first leg of the homeward route. About five minutes later, the rear gunner reported a single-engined fighter astern, and gave the captain directions for corkscrew manoeuvres, which were maintained for about ten minutes. The last time the rear gunner reported the fighter approaching, he gave no more directions, but I heard his guns open fire. Then a short burst from the fighter struck our fuselage. Immediately, we began to lose height. A fierce fire developed aft of the wireless op's position, and someone said that one or both of the starboard engines were hit. The captain ordered us to bale out. The aircraft was going down in a gradual dive, but it wasn't out of control. I tried to contact the mid-upper on intercom, but I got no reply, and made my way to the front escape-hatch. The air bomber jumped first, followed by the flight engineer and then me. It can't have been more than a minute after the captain gave the order. The wireless op. was standing behind me, ready to jump, and the captain had his 'chute on. I made a good landing in ploughed field."

It was assumed that the rear gunner, Sergeant Pickford, died in the combat, or was too badly injured to escape by parachute.

550 Squadron at North Killingholme despatched eighteen Lancasters, of which all but one returned. The missing aircraft was BQ H-Howe, which went down at Cheniers while in the deadly orbit over the assembly-point; the captain, Flight Lieutenant Grain, DFM, had been carrying a passenger - an officer of the Duke of Wellington's Regiment, seconded to North Killingholme for airfield defence duties. Major S. Whipp, TD, was not the only "brown job" to beg a ride with a bomber crew: he was one of the few to be with them when they died. Another 550 Squadron aircraft, flown by Flight Sergeant Lloyd, was badly damaged by a night-fighter; three of the crew were missing from the aircraft when Lloyd crash-landed it at a fighter base in Sussex.

BQ T-Tommy, captained by Sergeant Peter Marles, landed safely at North Killingholme. The crew's expectation that their tenth operation would be an easy one had been rudely shattered by the scene at the assembly-point, and by the flak opposition on their long-delayed bombing run. A shell in the starboard outer engine had started a fire, which Marles and the flight engineer had managed to extinguish. After de-briefing, the wireless operator, Alex Cleghorn, returned to the billet and, utterly exhausted, fell into his bed. Finding him there in the morning, his crew-mates silently carried both bed and occupant out of the Nissen hut, out of the domestic site, and as far as their strength and determination would allow. Awaking some time later, Cleghorn found himself alone, still wrapped in his blankets, in the middle of a field, and an object of interest to a herd of cows. It took him some time to orient himself, and even longer to appreciate the joke.

At Binbrook, 460 and 625 Squadrons, which had assigned most of their aircraft to attack the "special target", lost respectively five out of seventeen (there was one early return), and three out of sixteen. Few 460 Squadron crews heard any orders, either from the "1 Group Controller" or from Wing Commander Deane, and most dropped the bombs on their own initiative, their times-on-target ranging from H plus 8 minutes to H plus 29. AR R-Robert, flown by Warrant Officer Gritty, which had already been attacked by a night-fighter on the way to the target, was hit and set on fire by another over Châlons-sur-Marne at H plus 23; three of the crew either baled out, or were thrown clear of R-Robert when it exploded, and evaded capture. Pilot Officer Baker's AR J-Jig was hit on the bombing run and crashed a few miles north of the target. AR Z-Zebra Two, AR E-Easy and AR G-George, flown respectively by Pilot Officer Lloyd, Flight Sergeant Fry and Pilot Officer Smart, all of the

RAAF, were shot down to the south of the target, from which it can be inferred that they had made their bombing runs before they were destroyed. From these four aircraft there were no survivors.

Nine crews of 625 Squadron, hearing the order "All aircraft, bomb the red spot fires", abandoned the "special target" and joined the main attack. Of the three aircraft lost by the squadron, with no survivors, Pilot Officer Short's CF U-Uncle was destroyed on the bombing run, Pilot Officer McGaw's CF W-William three miles south of the target; the third, CF A-Apple, flown by a flight commander, Squadron Leader Gray, went down north-west of Sens, on the way back to the coast. A-Apple had been hit and set on fire by a night-fighter's cannon-shells, and the fuselage, aft of the flare-chute, had become an inferno. The rear gunner's only hope of survival would have been to jump at once. Sergeant Escritt, however, had stayed in the turret, giving his captain instructions for evasive action. "It's burning in the turret," had been his last words. "The flames are all around my arms." When the aircraft exploded, Squadron Leader Gray and the wireless operator, Sergeant Evans, had been flung into the night. One evaded capture, the other became a prisoner-of-war. The heroic rear gunner died with the other four members of A-Apple's crew.

The Special Duty Flight, leading those two squadrons on their lonely, ill-conceived mission, despatched five aircraft and lost AR J-Jig, flown by Flight Lieutenant Hull, DFC, who had flown one and one-third missions (under that strange edict) of a second tour. Three of his crew wore the ribbon of the DFM. It

Debris of 460 Sqn's AR-R (LM531), which crashed at Châlons-sur-Marne.

was Hull's voice which was heard above the target, handing over to his deputy with the words "I am hit and going down." The aircraft struck the ground near St. Remy-sous-Barbuise, eight miles south of the target, and the people of the village could only watch in horror while J-Jig and seven men were consumed by the flames.

Of the 1 Group squadrons, only No. 100, which had despatched eleven Lancasters from Waltham, with one abortive sortie, emerged physically unscathed from Mailly-le-Camp. The losses to the 5 Group squadrons, which had not been subjected to the same degree of mayhem over the assembly-point, were exactly half the number suffered by 1 Group. Only No. 50 Squadron at Skellingthorpe suffered on the same scale as the worst-hit 1 Group squadrons. Flying Officer Handley's VN I-Item, which came down at Poivres, was probably hit on the bombing run; Pilot Officer Hanson's VN P-Peter, from which only the wireless-operator, Sergeant Richardson, escaped, and VN U-Uncle, flown by Flight Lieutenant Blackham, DFC, fell a few miles south of the target; VN S-Sugar hit the ground some forty miles east-north-east of Paris, but whether Pilot Officer Dobson and his crew were still on the outbound route or, having bombed the target, were taking the shortest way home, is not possible to tell. 50 Squadron's loss-rate was over 25%, but such is the way the dice of life and death are cast that all twelve aircraft despatched by 61 Squadron, sharing the same base, made safe returns. One of these, flown by Pilot Officer Street, was on target at 0040 hours - thirty-six minutes later than its planned TOT - and must have been among the last to bomb.

Between them, Nos. 44 and 619 Squadrons at Dunholme Lodge contributed twenty-four aircraft to the operation. Pilot Officer Nolan's crew, in 44's KM K-King, were shot down over Dreux, forty-five miles west of Paris; Pilot Officer Wadsworth, DFC, of 619 Squadron, died with his crew when a night-fighter destroyed PG G-George, also on the homeward route, near Château-de-Thierry in the province of Aisne. A certain WAAF Intelligence Officer, de-briefing the returning crews, heard their descriptions of the scene above the target with rather more than professional concern. She knew that Leonard Cheshire's crews from Woodhall Spa had marked the target: one of them was her man and the mission sounded bad. She concentrated on completing the de-briefing, and tried to put Dave Shannon out of mind.

Of the other 5 Group squadrons, No. 207 lost two aircraft of the seventeen despatched (one suffered engine trouble and returned to Spilsby early). Both missing aircraft were shot down on the homeward route: Warrant Officer Lissette's EM F-Fox near Namours, as has been described, and EM M-Mike, with Pilot Officer Bell's crew, twenty-five miles east-south-east of Paris, also in Seine-et-Marne.

No. 9 Squadron despatched fifteen aircraft from Bardney, and fourteen made safe returns; two members of Flying Officer Ineson's crew survived when WS Y-Yoke was shot down over Normée, four miles south-west of the assembly-point, probably by a night-fighter while in the waiting orbit. The bomb-aimer, Flying Officer Porteous of the RNZAF, and the mid-upper gunner, Sergeant Chappell, baled out seconds before the aeroplane exploded; Porteous was held as a prisoner-of-war, while Chappell evaded capture and made his way back to England. Of the other crews, only Pilot Officer Lake's bombed on schedule. Flight Lieutenant Mathers and Pilot Officer Reeve dropped their bombs at twenty-six minutes to one - seven minutes after the attack should have ended.

Of twelve 57 Squadron aircraft and thirteen of 630 Squadron operating from East Kirkby, the only loss was No. 57's DX M-Mike, piloted by Flying Officer Scrivener, which crashed seventeen miles south-east of Paris on the journey home. All the crew were killed.

The Waddington squadrons, Nos. 463 and 467, had respectively despatched twelve and ten Lancasters, and one from each squadron failed to return. 463's JO G-George, with Flying Officer Fryer, RAAF, and his crew, went down at Poivres, just short of the target. 467's PO N-Nan, flown by Pilot Officer Dickson, also of the RAAF, hit the ground eighteen miles to the south, from which it can be assumed that Dickson's crew had completed their attack. Two escaped by parachute, and evaded capture, but Dickson and the others died when N-Nan hit the ground.

Main wheel of 460 Sqn's AR-R (LM531) at Châlons-sur-Marne.

Neither 49 Squadron at Fiskerton, with fourteen aircraft on the mission, nor No. 106 at Metheringham with twelve, incurred any losses, although two of No. 49's Lancasters were damaged. One of these aircraft, while approaching the target at 7,000 feet, was hit by a flak-burst, which filled the fuselage with smoke and decided the captain, Pilot Officer Ball, to jettison the bombs. No sooner had the load gone than a night-fighter's cannon shells destroyed the starboard outer engine and, among other damage, knocked out the intercom. Ball dived steeply and, although his aircraft was hit again, this time by machine-gun fire, which struck another engine, he eventually evaded the night-fighter's attentions and, with a dead starboard outer and the port outer giving half-power, limped home to Fiskerton. At some point in the action, both air gunners, hearing nothing on the intercom and probably assuming that their crew-mates had baled out, had themselves made their escape. Fiskerton listed them as prisoners-of-war.

The four Mosquitos of 617 Squadron flew back safely to Woodhall Spa, and all were on the ground by 0228 hours - over an hour before the Lancasters landed. When the news of their return was passed to Int/Ops at Dunholme Lodge, Section Officer Ann Shannon offered up a private prayer of thanks.

The squadrons at Coningsby suffered one loss each: No. 97, despatching nine aircraft, lost Flying Officer Ellesmere and his crew, when OF A-Able was shot down by a fighter sixteen miles east of Chartres on the homeward route. A-Able exploded when it hit the ground at two o'clock in the morning of Thursday, 4th May. The missing crew from 83 Squadron's ten was that of Squadron Leader Sparks, and Laurence Deane felt responsible for this: "I overlooked advising my deputy," he would write, "to follow my tactics for the return flight. He was one of those shot down - fortunately to survive."

Deane need not have blamed himself: the resourceful Sparks had every intention of taking the direct route back to Lincolnshire, and at low level. It was not a lack of know-how, but Sparks's dedication to his duty, that brought about his downfall. He had circled the target until he was satisfied that the attack, and so his responsibilities, were over. By that time, OL R-Robert had been in the area of Mailly-le-Camp for forty-five minutes and, as it transpired, that was just too long. Three months later, Sparks was to tell the operational researchers at Command HQ just what happened next.

"As I left the target, flying at 4,000 feet, I saw a fighter about 2,000 feet below me, and I began a succession of irregular evasive manoeuvres. The rear gunner and the visual air bomber were watching the fighter, and I could see it clearly myself in the moonlight each time I banked. After two or three minutes, while we were in a turn, the rear gunner and the air bomber lost sight of the fighter. Within a few seconds, a burst of cannon fire hit the starboard wing and it started to burn. At first I thought the fire was in the starboard outer engine, so I stopped it and feathered the propeller. Then I realised that the fire was in the number two petrol tank, between the starboard engines. The aircraft was vibrating violently and difficult to control. There was no word from the gunners after the attack, although the intercom was working, but I heard a groan just after feathering the engine. I never found out who it was because, at that moment, the whole wing from the fuselage to the starboard outer burst into flames. I gave the order to bale out. The visual air bomber jettisoned the front hatch and jumped out, followed by the flight engineer, the set-operator, the navigator and the wireless-op. I called the gunners on intercom and by flashing the call-lights, but there was no response. When I baled out myself, the aircraft was in an uncontrollable turn to starboard with three engines running. I don't know what height we were at."

As Sparks left the aircraft, so did the burning wing. It was then he discovered that his parachute-pack was only attached to the left clip of his harness. The clip and the strap, however, were enough to bear his weight, and his descent was ungainly, uncomfortable, but safe. He landed in a tree, some twenty-five north-west of the target, in the woodland between Montmirail and Epernay. All his crew survived, including the gunners, who, hearing his first order, had not lingered long. Two fell into enemy hands, but the rest avoided capture, and Sparks himself, with the aid of the Resistance, made his way to England and was back with his squadron a fortnight after D-Day.

The Mailly-le-Camp operation was over. Some three hundred and thirty Lancasters had reached the target area, and forty-two had been destroyed. Four men were missing from returning aircraft, and no-one would ever know their fate. Of the airmen who went down with the bombers, twenty-nine remained at liberty, and twenty-one were taken prisoner. Two hundred and fifty-five were dead.

Airmen's graves at Poivres.

CHAPTER EIGHT

PATRIOTS AND FRIENDS

When we left the crew of PH Q-Queenie, they were falling through the darkness towards the fertile farmland south of the target. Peter Maxwell, as the captain, had been the last to jump, and was still in free fall when he saw Q-Queenie flying on above him, like an airborne Marie Celeste. Then the port wing-tanks exploded, and the aircraft dived steeply. By the time he had pulled the D-ring (with his left hand) and the canopy had opened, Q-Queenie was a fiercely burning mass of wreckage on the ground. Maxwell made a good landing in open country near the village of La Belle Idée and, having buried his parachute and such pieces of his flying kit as he didn't think he'd need, he avoided the village and set off through the fields to find a safe resting place. He planned to make for the Spanish frontier, four hundred miles away, and he needed to conserve his physical resources.

Maurice Garlick, the navigator, who had preceded his pilot through the nose escape-hatch, was beginning to wonder if his fall would ever end (when descending by parachute at night, even in moonlight, it is difficult to judge your height above the ground), when his feet encountered some sort of linear obstruction - something that yielded, like a rope. Instantaneously, the night seemed to detonate. That was as much of his descent as he remembered: when consciousness returned, he was lying in a field and his left leg was hurting him a lot. He tried to rise, but his limbs would not respond. He was trembling violently, and tried to warm himself in the fabric of the parachute. Above him in the moonlight he saw the parallel lines of the power transmission cables and, through the physical trauma and the shock to his senses, realised what his feet had struck. "Garlick," he told himself, "you're lucky to be alive."

After a while, he opened his escape kit and ate two Horlicks tablets. That seemed to reactivate more of his senses, one of which reported the smell of scorched flesh. He took off his flying boots, and slit the sleeves of his battle-dress trousers to the hip. Both his legs were covered in abrasions and blisters: the left from sole to thigh, and the right, which was numb, from the ankle to the calf. He tore a silk panel from the parachute canopy and bandaged the injuries as securely as he could, then he lay back in the moonlight, huddled in the canopy, and slept.

If Garlick's survival from contact with the power line was remarkable, the escape of a nineteen year-old rear gunner, Sergeant Jack Worsfold, as it has been reported, must be regarded as miraculous. His aircraft, 101 Squadron's Z-Zebra, had been riddled by bullets on the bombing run, and the starboard outer engine set ablaze. Through a babel on the intercom, he heard the voice of his pilot - "Bale out, bale out!" He opened the doors of his turret, crawled into the fuselage and, taking his parachute-pack from its stowage, found to his dismay that it was ripped to shreds. The Messerschmitt came in again. It seemed to Worsfold that the Lancaster disintegrated. Then, still on his hands and knees in the rear section of the fuselage, he was falling - falling free. He felt a hard blow in the ribs, a pain in his hand, and that was all. His next recollection was of lying in a gorse bush, and the bush was smouldering. He had fallen for 7,500 feet, hit the high-tension cables, bounced from them into a fir tree and dropped into the bush. He had fractures of the thigh, shoulder, three ribs and two fingers; the flesh of his face and chest was burned. A section of Z-Zebra's fuselage lay fifty yards away. Thanks to that magic carpet, to a French village doctor and, after he was captured, to the staff of a German military hospital, Worsfold lived to tell the tale.

Although John Ackroyd, of 192 Squadron's DT V-Victor, made a more orthodox landing, it was not entirely trouble-free. Later, he recalled those moments of descent:

> "One of my straps broke and I came down lop-sided. I came down rather quickly, too, because part of the canopy was torn. I don't know how that happened. With a three-quarter moon, it was nearly like day, and I could see I was heading for trees, but I could do nothing about it. Actually, the trees broke my fall - and in such a way that I was hanging about two feet above the ground. I pressed the harness release and dropped down. The 'chute was stuck firmly in the tree, and try as I would the thing wouldn't come down. In the end I gave it up as a bad job, and moved some distance away to the shelter of some shrubs. I rested under them for a short while, to try and think things out. In the distance I heard the barking of dogs, and I thought 'Oh, God! They're after me already'."

No dogs were seeking him; the countryside was still. When dawn broke on Thursday 4th May, he discovered a barn, slept there for a while and then approached the farmhouse. Half-an-hour later, refreshed by ersatz coffee, wearing cast-off clothes and boots, he was on his way. Like Peter Maxwell, he set his course for Spain.

All he knew of his crew-mates was that Sergeant Cottrell had died in the aircraft, and it would be some years before he discovered what had happened to the rest. The rear gunner, Sergeant Burton, in fact, had failed to survive the parachute descent: in his fall, he had struck high tension cables, as had Garlick and Worsfold, but for Burton the contact had probably been fatal. His body was found later, impaled on a fence-post in a park at Villeret. Sergeant Preece, the navigator, had dropped into a lake between the villages of Morvilliers and Epothémont, and it was only the Welshman's powerful physique that had enabled him, still in his flying kit, to swim to the bank. After that exertion and several hours of walking, with no idea of his direction, fatigue overtook him. As luck would have it, the garden in which he chose to fall asleep was that of Monsieur Dormont, who was strongly sympathetic to the Allied cause. Meanwhile, Sergeant Stormont, the mid-upper gunner, having made a safe landing near Soulaines-Dhuys village, arrived, again by good fortune, at a house where he was welcomed by Monsieur Bertin, a World War I veteran, his wife Claudia, and their two teen-age children, Jeanne and Bernard. Madame

Bertin was a tiny, blue-eyed lady, intensely patriotic, who spoke the English language and was also, it transpired, a formidable organiser. Within a matter of hours, Preece and Stormont were reunited in her home.

Some fifteen miles to the west, Maurice Garlick had awoken, still wrapped in his parachute, at four in the morning. He was a Londoner, thirty-one years old, and, by nature, methodical and cautious. Some men, in his position, might have decided that their over-riding need was for medical attention, and that it mattered little whether they obtained it from the Germans or the French. This consideration did not cross Garlick's mind. His only purpose was to evade capture and to find his way back home. He was worried by the thought that, in due course, someone would arrive to investigate the failure in the power supply - some official, perhaps, who would promptly hand him over to the occupying forces. Recollecting the "Escape and Evasion" teaching back at Wickenby that all incriminating items should be promptly buried, he oriented himself by his escape-kit compass,

Sergeant Stormont, Wireless Operator in a Halifax of 192 Sqn's DT-V.

and began to crawl south-east towards the nearest corner of the field. There he dug a pit with his jack-knife and buried the parachute-harness with what remained of the canopy. He decided to retain his Mae West - the inflatable life-jacket - in case he had to cross a stretch of water, and continued south-eastwards on his hands and knees. Neither river nor stream impeded his progress, but a railway track did, on a steep embankment, from the top of which he saw, about two miles away and more or less on course, an inviting copse of trees. That, he decided, must be his next objective, but the climb up the embankment had exhausted his strength, and he crawled into a cabbage-patch to take another rest. The sound of voices wakened him - the voices of ploughmen encouraging their horses in a nearby field. It was his instinct to approach them, but another piece of teaching from the lectures at Wickenby made him pause. "Don't reveal yourself to people in a group," he remembered, "wait until you find one man alone."

It so happened that while Garlick was hiding in his cabbage-patch, and the rest of Q-Queenie's crew, each unaware of where the others were, were keeping their heads down not a million miles away, the commander of the unit which had brought about their downfall was standing at attention, wearing No. 1 uniform, in Hitler's "Eagle's Nest" at Berchtesgaden. The Knight's Cross worn by Maior Wilhelm Herget, Commanding I Gruppe of Nachtjagdgeschwader 4, victor of forty-nine combats by night and nineteen by day, would henceforth be augmented by the highly-prized Oak Leaves, personally awarded by his Führer, along with a smile, a handshake and that well-known flick of the wrist which passed for a salute, while the Luftwaffe chief, Reichsmarschall Hermann Göring, beamed his fat approval.

That evening, as dusk fell over Aube, Garlick fortified himself with another Horlicks tablet and continued his journey, moving more painfully as the numbness in his right leg started to wear off, until he reached what he guessed was the main road running south-east from Romilly to Troyes, and which he crossed in a break between processions of military traffic. Dawn on Friday brought a shower of rain, some of which he collected in the lid of his ration tin and stored in the escape-kit water container. He ate the kit's ration of processed chocolate and cheese, augmented by a handful of grass, and dozed the day away.

That night the notion came to him to cut two branches from a hedgerow with which to make a pair of crutches. It was then that he realised he had buried the jack-knife along with his parachute. His nail-file was not the best of substitutes, but eventually, and for the first time since he landed in France, Garlick stood erect and tried to walk. The instant pain knocked him flat upon his back. Two further efforts convinced him that, however he might travel, it would not be by walking. He constructed a sling for his left foot from the parachute cord and, helped by that and his crutches, reached his objective by daybreak on Saturday. The copse, at close quarters, proved disappointingly small, with very little cover, and he hobbled grimly on. He needed shelter - a barn, perhaps, a lean-to or a shed. Not far off his course, a small hill seemed to offer the sort of panoramic view which might reveal a farmhouse with the buildings he was seeking. When he had struggled halfway to the top, a Ju-88 roared low above his head. In the fugitive, the belief is strong that all the world is hunting him - sufficiently strong to dim the light of reason - and Garlick was convinced that the Ju-88 was after him. He threw himself into a clump of bushes on the hillside and stayed there, trembling, until the daylight faded.

Meanwhile, to the east, in the area of Brienne-le-Château, John Ackroyd had found another farmhouse and, once more, had tried his luck (neither he, nor any of the airmen on the run, were to know that, on that day, the Gestapo had put a price of 25,000 francs upon their heads). Ackroyd's luck had held:

"The farmer's wife took off my boots and bathed my feet, disregarding the smell (a full day's walking in tight boots - pooh!). They were preparing the evening meal, so I guessed it must gave been about seven or seven-thirty. There were children, but I don't remember how many. The farmer had two black eyes and his face was cut. That had been done by the Boche at the market the day before. I ate the meal with them, and then I was given a bed in a room to myself. I don't remember a bed so comfortable. I didn't wake until mid-afternoon. That would have been Friday 6th May.

A man came to see me - I think he was the local Mayor - and said that on the following morning he would come with two bicycles (which had to be looked after with care as they were very precious), and he would lead me to the house of a person who would help me. He made sure I had no identification - no RAF clothes, no labels. I had francs, and that was OK, but I had to leave my escape maps at the farm. He said they would be returned later, but they never were."

While remaining unaware of Ackroyd's adventures, or indeed of Garlick's or of any of the others' (even the next-of-kin had heard no more than "Missing in action"), people in Britain at least knew something of the mission which had occasioned their involuntary exile in the Champagne countryside. The Mailly-le-Camp attack had, after all, made a front page story in the Friday morning papers.

The headline in The Daily Mail (price one penny) was "RAF SMASH AT MASSED TANKS - First Blow at the 'Fortress Army' - LUFTWAFFE FORCED INTO BATTLE", followed by a column of reportage, in tiny wartime print, which included these paragraphs: "Bomber Command has struck the first great blow at Hitler's anti-invasion armies massed in France in the 'Fortress of Europe'. On Wednesday night a 1,500-tons attack was launched on the military depot at Mailly, where large numbers of German tanks and military vehicles, expressly marshalled to fight on a wide stretch of the enemy's western lines, are believed to have been destroyed. This attack met strong fighter opposition, and may have precipitated a pre-invasion aerial battle of the night, fought out not only between fighters and bombers but also by the fighters of both sides."

A reader who refused to be distracted by such adjacent column headings as "BLACK MARKET IN HOUSEMAIDS - MPs Lash Wealthy 'Servant

Hoarders'", "RED ARMY AGAIN ON THE MOVE", "Mosquito Got 4 in 6 Minutes" and "BBC USE WRONG RECORD", or even by a Food Ministry recipe for making pancakes with dried eggs, would observe, perhaps with the aid of a magnifying glass, that "The RAF's loss of 49 aircraft during the night must be regarded as above the average for all forms of bomber operations." The Daily Express made the Mosquito item its main news story, followed by the housemaid exposé, "INVASION BEHIND SCHEDULE - Goebbels", and "CURTIN: You're all welcome to Australia", with "PARKED PANZERS SMASHED BY RAF" in fourth position. Under the banner headline "MOONRIDER GETS FOUR", the air correspondent described a successful sortie by an intruder pilot, Wing Commander Goodman, DFC, over Dijon on the Thursday evening. "All of them went down very satisfactorily", the hero was quoted as remarking. (Where were you, Moonrider, when the bomber boys needed you on Wednesday night?)

"PANZER DEPOT HIT BY 1,500 TONS - RAF BOMBERS MAKE 'INVASION RAID' - FIERCE MOONLIGHT AIR BATTLES OVER FRANCE" were the headlines to this story in The Daily Telegraph:

"Fleets of Luftwaffe night fighters were thrown into battle in a determined attempt to hold off the RAF assault, but they failed. Reconnaissance had shown a huge concentration of tanks and lorries at Mailly, clearly part of the preparations being made to defend the West Wall. The depot was raised to a high priority on the target list and a strong bomber force despatched at the first opportunity. The attack, obviously linked with the approaching invasion, provoked a violent German reaction in brilliant moonlight with excellent visibility over the whole area.

As soon as the Pathfinders had laid their marking flares the battle began. Fighter flares were dropped, and in the eerie combination of flares, fires, flak and moonlight the bombers streamed in to deliver their loads.

Veteran crews said the fighting was the fiercest in their experience. Combats raged over the target itself and for 40 miles on the homeward journey. RAF losses totalled 49 aircraft from all operations, which included sea-mining.

Bombers from one base [this was probably Wickenby - Author] claimed two enemy planes destroyed and one damaged.

The moonlight enabled pilots to see their big bombs burst right on the target. Huge fires began, spread and were then hidden by vast clouds of smoke…"

Aiming point photo taken by Norman Barker of Browning's crew in 103 Sqn's PM-U.

In the province of Aube, meanwhile, Maurice Garlick's improvised foot-sling was giving more trouble than was warranted by the easement of his suffering and, once on the move again, he settled for a mixed regime of hobbling and crawling. Reaching a cart-track, he settled down beside it to smoke the remaining shreds of his tobacco. As though they had been waiting for that moment, a troop of German soldiers cycled up the track. Thrusting his pipe into the undergrowth, Garlick tried to melt into the scenery. The soldiers, looking neither right nor left, passed by. The sense of relief awakened his appetite and, foraging around him, he unearthed a few potatoes and some wild rhubarb stalks. Not entirely sated by this, he chewed a Benzedrine pill, which he immediately regretted, so loudly did it cause his heart to thump. When the palpitations ceased, he travelled on, in fits and starts. In the afternoon, the tower of Troyes cathedral came in view, and navigator Garlick, for the first time in three days, was sure of his position.

At 11 o'clock in the morning of Sunday 7th May, still moving imperceptibly south-east, he found the sort of farmhouse for which he had been seeking. He hid behind a hawthorn bush and kept watch until, just after midday, a grey-haired man, wearing a smock and a beret, emerged from an outbuilding and set to work with horse and plough in the neighbouring field. Garlick watched him, trying to make his mind up, for another two hours. He knew that this approach had got to be the right one. If the Frenchman were no patriot, no friend to the Allies, and simply summoned the soldiers, there was nothing he could do about it: he could neither flee nor fight. At last he crawled forward, as the ploughman neared his hiding place, and raised his hand. "Bonjour, Monsieur," he called.

The Frenchman started, glanced at Garlick, then carefully ploughed another pair of furrows. When he returned, he looked the airman up and down with a lift of the eyebrows, and Garlick realised that, with his five-day growth of beard and tattered clothing, he was not a pretty sight. "Pardonnez moi, Monsieur," he said, "je suis un aviateur Anglais. Est-ce que vous êtes le propriétaire de cette ferme cela?"

The Frenchman inclined his head, with his eyes still on the airman.

"S'il vous plaît, Monsieur," continued Garlick, "j'ai soif. Aussi, j'ai faim." He accompanied these words with appropriate gestures, and the farmer seemed to catch his drift. Motioning Garlick back into his hiding place, he trudged slowly to the farmhouse and returned, some minutes later, with a mug of home-made cider. Soon, Garlick was eating eggs, cheese and bread with the family - the farmer (whom he gathered was a widower), a daughter and son-in-law. He requested a solution of salt and hot water in which to bathe his legs, but the cupboard was bare of salt, and they made do with disinfectant. Then, he was shaved, and dressed in a curious costume from the farmer's wardrobe comprising an ancient tweed jacket, a pair of striped city trousers and a felt hat. Tentatively, he enquired about the prospect of a few days' bed and board, at which the family shook their heads. Too dangerous, they said, the Boche was everywhere. Where, they asked, did he propose to go? "South-south-west," he told them, "I intend to walk to Spain." Again, Gallic eyebrows were raised. They gave him such food as remained on the table and a replacement for his jack-knife. As an afterthought, he filled the inflatable collar of his Mae West with cider. They refused the francs from his escape-kit, but accepted - as a souvenir - an English one pound note.

Once he had hobbled out of sight of the farm house, Garlick - in whose character fortitude and caution were equally combined - made an easterly detour over many fields before resuming his course, alternately on sticks and on his hands and knees, sleeping in copses, for six more days and nights.

When the cider was exhausted, he begged a glass of water from a woman attending to her garden, and would have asked for help had not something in her manner put him off.

On the evening of Sunday 14th May, by now very weak and only moving from memory, he came to a farmhouse standing by itself, off the main road west of Troyes, near the village of Bucey-en-Othe. A teen-age boy, who was working with a plough, quickly piercing Garlick's disguise, pronounced him an evader, and said he would be fed if he went to the farmhouse. In imagination, Garlick saw a kitchen table, food and drink, a chair. He began to make his painful way towards the house. Then he stopped, and turned back to the youth. "Il y a un ruisseau, peut-être? Il faut que je me - er - raser."

Five minutes later, he was sitting in the envisioned chair and the farmer's "femme de ménage" was setting out what he had come to realise was the staple menu of bread, cheese and cider. "You are in good hands now," said the youth, joining Garlick at the table, and confided that he, too, was in hiding at the farm to avoid deportation to a German labour camp.

The farmer, whose name was Charles Decreon, had watched Garlick closely as he hobbled through the yard. As a serving soldier when France was overrun, he had been imprisoned in Normandy, and very nearly starved. It was not until the German Army itself had needed grain that he had been released from the prison camp and sent back to work his farm. On arriving there, he had found three strangers working in his fields. "These new men," he had asked his wife, "did you take them on?"

"But of course," she had replied, "someone had to plough the land."

"Very well. But why are they wearing my clothes?"

"Because they are escaped prisoners, and their dress was unsuitable for farm-work." Willy-nilly, Decreon had taken the first step on the road that was to lead him into the heart of the Resistance. Many a stranger, in the last three years, had knocked upon his door: few had been invited and many had not been what they seemed. There had been gendarmes and militia, Maquisards and men of the Resistance, German SS and infantry troops, escapees and evaders of several nationalities. Decreon had dealt with every one of them, according to their needs, and sent them on their way. He would deal with this visitor, who had limped in on two sticks, dressed like a scarecrow, just as he had with all the rest. Bending his head to avoid the lintel, he walked into the kitchen.

Garlick, looking up, saw a powerfully-built man, with a broad, friendly face and wide-set blue eyes - a man, Garlick judged, some ten years older than himself. As they surveyed each other, they heard the sound of a vehicle entering the yard. Decreon spoke to the teenager. "Cache-le dans l'autre pièce pendant que je m'occupe des Boches."

In the yard, four German soldiers were standing by an Army truck. The Feldwebel beckoned. "Have you seen anything unusual, Frenchman? Any strangers?"

Decreon shrugged his shoulders, and spoke in the German he had learned in the prison camp. "Nothing to speak of. Things are very quiet. Would you and your men care to come into the house? A glass of cider, perhaps?"

"No, we are busy. Keep your eyes open, and report any strangers instantly."

Decreon returned to the house, and opened the door into the back-room. Garlick was slumped on the floor. "Our visitor has fainted," said the youth. "I think his strength has gone."

"Then let him eat and drink."

When Garlick had recovered, he ate like the starving man he was. "Merci beaucoup, Monsieur," he said, when he had finished the meal, and laid some notes on the table.

"You are English?" asked Decreon.

Garlick nodded.

"But this is French money. How is that?"

Cautious as ever, Garlick hid the truth. "The people who first helped me," he said, "changed my pounds for francs."

"I think he is genuine," said the teenager in French. "He shaved in the stream before entering the house."

Decreon chuckled. "You have convinced me. Only an Englishman would do that." He folded the notes and gave them back to Garlick. "At this time of year," he said, "the Boche agricultural overseer snoops around constantly. It's not possible that you stay here. We'll clean you up and move you on. Don't worry, you'll be with true patriots and friends."

John Ackroyd, too, had found himself among friends. In the village of Piney, to which his guide had led him on the precious bicycles, he was given new clothes, a pair of boots that fitted, an indigenous beret and as much food and drink as he could comfortably consume. It was during the course of a lively party in the market square, that Marcel Doré, who, he gathered, was the local knacker, arrived in a lorry to transport him to Montmoret.

"In the lorry, which was powered by charcoal gas, I sat in the cab between Marcel and another man who worked as his butcher. (Later, I saw this man slit the throat of a calf and drink the blood as it ran out.) We pulled into the back of the Gendarmerie to pick up some animal feed - black market, I presumed - and had a drink with the gendarmes. Then we stopped to see the end of a football match and had a few more drinks with the players. When we finally set off for Marcel's home, we were stopped by three German soldiers who wanted a lift into Troyes. They got in the back, and we dropped them off at the end of Marcel's drive. When we got into the house I was introduced to the other six airmen who were there - five Americans and another Englishman."

Monsieur Doré, it transpired, not only dealt legitimately in carcases and hides, but conducted a busy undercover trade in pig, sheep and calf meat. By way of a side-line, he converted animal fat into a marketable soap. When, however, a German soldier knocked upon the door, seeking to purchase a bar or two of this

Maurice Garlick and his wife during a post-war visit to Estissac.

commodity, he was brusquely told that there was none for sale. Piqued, perhaps, by the refusal, the soldier, on departure, hijacked Doré's donkey. The indignant dealer promptly drove to Troyes and complained to the Commandant. The donkey was returned.

From Bucey, meanwhile, a car had taken Maurice Garlick twelve miles north-east to Ossey-les-Trois-Maisons, where a middle-aged Frenchwoman, assisted by her daughter, put him straight to bed, promising that a doctor would attend him in the morning. For this assurance Garlick, whose legs were showing signs of putrefaction, offered up a heartfelt word of thanks before he fell asleep. Early next day, the doctor, who did not reveal his name, examined Garlick's burns, doused them with surgical spirit and covered them with bandages. For the next five days, while Madamoiselle stayed indoors, feigning illness, to justify the doctor's visits, the treatment was repeated, which was no fun for Garlick: each time the bandages were removed it caused his wounds to open and his eyes to water. To give the doctor his due, he refused all offers of payment for his services, as did the ladies who nursed him faithfully throughout.

Then came bad news: in the environs of Troyes, the Gestapo had arrested a member of the local Resistance, along with four Allied airmen whom he had been sheltering. It had to be assumed that, under interrogation, he would inevitably reveal the names of other members of France's secret army, and that meant death or, at best, deportation. Madame and Madamoiselle would face whatever was to come, but they would face it with more confidence if Garlick were not lying upstairs in the bedroom. The car was recalled, another house found, and another two brave Frenchwomen; the same nameless doctor reappeared, however, remorselessly to continue his agonising treatment.

That Troyes Resistance leader, the news of whose arrest had spread throughout the underground, was Marcel Doré. His home in Montmoret had been standing in danger of becoming overcrowded, and he had planned, at the weekend, to move two of his lodgers to another "safe house". Ackroyd was one who had prepared himself to go.

"On Thursday May 12th, a civilian arrived. Marcel didn't know him, but he had papers showing he was with a Resistance group some distance away. He was here to confirm the number of Allied airmen in the Troyes area, and to make arrangements to get us back to England. That evening, as we were eating our meal, the house was surrounded by soldiers. The Gestapo entered with the same civilian who had come in the morning, and more soldiers. Two of the Americans, who were nearest to the door, managed to get to a hidey-hole under the house. The rest of us were arrested. Marcel and his friend were beaten up, but we weren't harmed at that stage. The two Americans who had hidden were caught next day when they were trying to get away."

An airman in uniform, captured by the enemy, would probably be told "For you, the war is over", and in due course be confined in a POW camp. That was bad enough, but not so unpleasant as what was liable to occur if he were dressed in civilian clothes. Such a captive would be regarded as a spy and, if anything were left worth a bullet when the Gestapo had done with him, he could, quite properly, be shot. Ackroyd and his comrades were to suffer many hardships in two civil prisons - firstly in Paris and, a week later, in Frankfurt-am-Main. The sufferings of Marcel Doré, their gallant protector, were not to be protracted. En route to the infamous concentration camp at Dachau, packed into a cattle-truck - a hideous irony - he died of suffocation.

At the home of the Bertins in Soulaines-Dhuys, Preece and Stormont had been joined by Tom Munro, the special operator in their Halifax crew, and by Bob Sherman, an American fighter pilot who had landed by parachute within the last few days. The bodies of Cottrell, still dressed in shreds of Jim Carpenter's flying kit, and of Burton had meanwhile been buried in the small graveyard at la Ville-aux-Bois, where a large congregation, including the Mayors of nearby villages and a German funeral party from the garrison in Troyes, had attended the interment. Preece and Stormont, on being told of this, had been greatly moved, but it had worried them to learn that the bunches of flowers placed upon the graves by little Jeanne and Bernard Bertin had been conspicuously tied in French tricolour ribbon.

Claudia Bertin's plan was to pass her four evaders on to an underground group at Mussy-Grancey, on the border of the Côte d'Or, some thirty miles to the south. They were to travel in pairs: Stormont and Munro via Essoyes, Preece and Sherman via Cunfin. The first two were hunted, hid for days below the floor boards of a château and remained at large. Preece and Sherman were captured as they approached a farm that was to have been their refuge. They, like Ackroyd, would be starved and beaten to make them give information - information that wasn't theirs to give.

In the days that followed the Gestapo coup in Troyes, Maurice Garlick's latest resting place steadily accumulated an influx of evaders, one of whom - a fluent French-speaker - having convinced himself of Garlick's bona fides, informed him that, when the Allied troops invaded, all RAF men in the local area were to gather in a wood near la Lisière-des-Bois, sixteen miles south-west of Troyes. There they would form themselves into a sabotage force under the command of the senior officer in the locality - one Flight Lieutenant Foley (who was, as it happened, the set-operator from the crew of Squadron Leader Sparks) - and do what they could to harass the enemy. Since Garlick was still quite unable to walk, he found it hard to see himself in the role of a saboteur, and the information failed to excite him. He was more concerned by a report that a Gestapo unit was about to conduct a search through the village, and was relieved to be rapidly returned to Charles Decreon's farmhouse near Bucey, where he had made his first contact with "patriots and friends".

His stay there was brief: on the evening of Friday 26th May, in a new suit of clothes, a pair of carpet slippers and the inevitable beret, he was escorted by a local shopkeeper, one Marcel Dupont, to the village of Estissac, four miles to the west, on the road from Troyes to Sens. Whether Dupont was the ideal escort under the circumstances must be open to doubt, for he insisted upon stopping at each café en route in order to demonstrate, to all with eyes to see, that their neighbourhood hosier was the sort of man who was entrusted with the safe conduct of a real live English airman.

Despite Dupont's digressions, they reached their destination. Estissac was a small community, set amidst the fields of maize and sunflowers whose product afforded its inhabitants their major source of income. A hundred or so cottages and substantial square-built houses were grouped around a fine town hall (the "Mairie") and a picturesque covered market place. A clear, sun-dappled stream bubbled through the village on its way to join the Seine, and above the water a platform hung suspended on a system of pulleys, by means of which it was adjusted to accord with variations in the level of the stream. There, the housewives of Estissac would congregate on wash-days, exchanging village gossip, and scrubbing and rinsing without recourse to artificial aids.

At the end of a lane between the stream and the market place stood the residence of the local postman, Joseph Lebrun. As was not uncommon in French houses of the period, only the front wall was furnished with windows, all of which were shuttered. Although this tended to darken the interior, it provided a high degree of privacy for the family Lebrun and their occasional visitors. The first-storey room in which Garlick, once fed, was put to bed, had no windows, and its door was concealed by a large walnut wardrobe. Flight Lieutenant Foley, who now arrived upon the scene, saw it as his duty to stand by downstairs in order to accept the gifts of cigarettes and foodstuffs which were brought to the door by well-meaning villagers. Monsieur Lebrun, who had a wife and five daughters to support (and another child expected), was glad of the gifts but didn't care for the publicity, as he also happened to be the leader of the local Resistance. Foley, appreciating the problem, moved on to join forces with other members of the secret army, while Lebrun, who had been a medical orderly in the first World War, shook his head and tut-tutted about the state of Garlick's legs. Two days later, the Maquis' own doctor appeared, and prescribed the saline solution which, some three weeks earlier, had been Garlick's own suggestion, and antiseptic powder. Under this treatment, applied daily by Lebrun, Garlick's condition steadily improved, and his morale received a boost when, in the mid-afternoon of 29th May, as he dozed in an armchair in his hidden room, the wardrobe was shifted, the door was opened and he heard a voice he knew. "Wakey, wakey, Maurice, you idle man!" He looked up. Standing beside him, dressed like a bandit in a Wild West movie and grinning broadly, was Q-Queenie's bomb-aimer, Paddy O'Hara.

While that reunion was taking place in Estissac, the armies of the Allies, thronging the Channel ports and the coastal towns of southern England, were preparing to embark on the greatest sea-borne onslaught in the history of warfare. There could be no concealment of the force that was assembled: fifty thousand men to assault the beaches, two million more to follow them ashore, with their armament and vehicles, supplies and ammunition. Two thousand vessels would form the great armada; eleven thousand aircraft would fly in their support - bombers and fighters to attack the defences, transports and gliders to drop troops behind the beaches. Throughout the month of May, loads of arms and ammunition were being dropped into France to supply the secret army, and three-man SOE teams were parachuting in to establish liaison with the local leaders.

The plan for "Overlord" had existed in outline since the summer of 1943, and the German High Command knew that well enough. Everyone knew the invasion was coming, and those who studied tide-charts could make a good guess as to when. The problem for the enemy was where. Generalfeldmarschall Erwin Rommel, whom Hitler had appointed to inspect and improve the defences in the west, agreed with his Führer (always a prudent posture to adopt) that the Allies would favour the beaches of Normandy. The Western Commander, Generalfeldmarschall von Rundstedt, however, took a different view: he believed that, since the Pas de Calais area offered the shortest sea crossing and the straightest route to Germany, the choice would fall there. Wherever it fell, both sides were aware that "Overlord" would decide the outcome of the war. If it were to fail, the losses to the Allies might cripple them for years, and the full might of the Reich could be hurled against the Russians, while its development of jet aircraft, guided missiles and long-range submarines could proceed apace; if it succeeded, Germany must inevitably fall - crushed between the Allies and the Red Army.

At that time, the German Army's divisions were dispersed all over Europe: there were a hundred and sixty-three on the eastern front, twenty-one in the Balkans, twenty-six in Italy, twelve in Norway, nine in the Fatherland and fifty-eight in the west, of which eight were in Mediterranean France and the remainder arrayed along the thousand miles of coastline from the Hook of Holland to the frontier of Spain. Those western divisions, however, which numbered fifty-eight on paper, amounted in reality to less than twenty-five, just as the "Atlantic Wall" was only a wall in Hitler's imagination. His Feldmarschalls knew that they needed at least one division for every five miles of coastline: what they had was a tenth of that force. It was only in the Pas de Calais, at von Rundstedt's insistence, that the defences equated with the propaganda strength.

As for Normandy, the best that Rommel could do there was to augment the minefields, intensify the training and build up the weapon-stocks. The most important preparation, however, was to locate the armoured reserve, and there he had a problem: the bulk of the Panzers, by the High Command's edict, formed an inner defence ring, lying in a rectangle far from the coast.

Rommel believed that the battle for Europe would be fought on the beaches. Lose that, lose the war. All he had to fight with on those beaches were three infantry divisions entrenched along the coastline, another - the 91st Division, with its parachute regiment - far out on the left, and an armoured division on the right, close to Caen. That division, it so happened, was the 21st Panzer from Mailly-le-Camp.

CHAPTER NINE

JACK CRIGHTON'S STORY

When an RAF airman of World War II pulled the D-ring of his parachute, and the main canopy deployed, he was liable to receive two simultaneous, physical impressions. The first, which was illusory, and only occurred if the straps of his harness were not absolutely tight, was that his behind had split in two; the second, which was real, was that one or both of his boots had fallen off - especially if he happened to be wearing the old-fashioned pull-on type without laces. Sergeant Jack Crighton, whose last act in Q-Queenie had been to clip a parachute-pack to his pilot's harness - albeit upside down - was fortunate in this: he only lost one boot. What follows is his description of the subsequent events in the words he used himself.

"I got my 'chute together and found a place to conceal it, then put some distance between me and the spot where I had landed, and found a small copse in which to hide. It was a long night and I ate some of my emergency rations when I felt a bit peckish. When daylight came I saw a French family working in a field nearby, but I had to wait for nightfall to approach a young man who was still around when the rest had gone. He didn't seem all that surprised. He exclaimed 'RAF' and motioned for me to lay low. He returned later and beckoned to me to follow him. I asked him where I was and he said 'Villacerf'. It was dark by the time he took me near water and we got into a flat-bottomed punt, but after a few minutes we got out and he took me to a house. I was given a meal but everyone was very wary. I found out that the Germans had used this ploy so they were taking no chances. I spent the night there and next morning I was off early aboard a cattle truck with a cow and three Frenchmen who were walking arsenals. They milked the cow and gave me a drink. I remember going through a large town and the French boys were on the look-out. I found later this was a garrison town called Troyes.

After many miles we stopped at a village called la Lisière-des-Bois - the edge of the woods. I was greeted by a Frenchman who spoke excellent English. He was M. Marcel Deriveri and he had spent some time in England. He took me to his home by a devious route along back lanes. It was a nice cottage. I met his young wife who spoke no English but was very pleasant. During the next few days three more airmen arrived, among them Jim Davidson, our mid-upper gunner. It was obvious we would have to move, and within a few days one of the resistance boys came and we were off, this time to the forests - the Forêt d'Othe - to join a Maquis.

We nearly froze the first few nights as we had no shelter. We were the first of a Maquis formation which swelled considerably during the next few days. Our rear gunner, Bert Townsend, turned up next, so we three shared one blanket, and took turns to sleep in the middle."

It transpired that the thirty-two year old Londoner, Sergeant Townsend, when he baled out of Q-Queenie, had landed safely on a woodland road near the little town of Romilly-sur-Seine. His first bad moment had come when

Sergeants Davison, Crighton, and others. at la Lisière-des-Bois.

three German tanks, with searchlights blazing, had lumbered towards him through the trees. In the same way that Ackroyd was unnerved by barking dogs, and as Garlick would be later by the Ju-88, Townsend was convinced that the enemy had come to hunt him down. He had hidden in the bushes until dawn; then, notwithstanding the Wickenby lecturer's advice, he had approached a group of farmhands working on the land. Their reaction had been cordial: they had selected a reasonably dry ditch for him to hide in and indicated an intention to send help. Townsend had composed himself to wait. Sure enough, at five o'clock that evening, a gendarme had appeared who, having questioned him closely, had provided a bicycle, a civilian suit and a night's accommodation in Troyes. Four days later, Q-Queenie's rear gunner had joined forces with the Maquis in the expanse of woodland, some thirty miles in length, which lay south of the main road from Troyes to Sens and was called the Forêt d'Othe .

      "We took our turn at guard duty," Crighton's story continued, "even though we were in the forest. One day about three weeks later I was on guard when I heard a shot and Bert came running to tell me that Jim was shot and was calling for me. I rushed back and found him on the ground, shot through the thigh. He had been shot accidentally by a young Frenchman cleaning his rifle. The hole of entry was small but the exit hole was a real mess. He had a smashed pelvis and he had gone grey with shock. I found one part of the bullet stuck in his shirt so I assumed that it had hit the bone. They took him away to seek medical care, but they told me later that he had died. The young Frenchman had a rough passage with the other resistance boys and I told the chief, Pierre, that it was time they learned to treat firearms with respect.

During this time, I noticed Pierre listening to the radio at certain times of the day and especially at 9 o'clock. I asked what the interest was, and he eventually told me that a certain message was broadcast to announce the various parachute drops. Each message meant a different dropping zone and he said one was imminent. The message was "La guêpe est dans le sac à couchage" - 'The wasp is in the sleeping bag'. If the message was repeated at 9 o'clock the drop was on. The dropping zone was a clearing about 2 kilometres from our camp. It came through at 9 o'clock and we were on our way. I was stationed at one corner of the field with a Maquis boy and a Bren gun. It was after midnight when the Halifax dropped its load of arms. They consisted of Bazookas, Brens, Colt 45s and plastic explosive. There were no luxuries, only weapons and I believe a couple of small radio receivers. On the second parachutage I attended, two agents were dropped but they were whisked off a bit smartish before any of the 'Anglais' had a chance to speak to them."

Eleven days after the raid on Mailly-le-Camp, the final "Overlord" plan was presented at a meeting in London attended by General Dwight D. Eisenhower as Supreme Allied Commander, Air Chief Marshal Sir Arthur Tedder as his deputy, General Sir Bernard Montgomery as the Ground Force Commander, Admiral Sir Bertram Ramsay as C.-in-C. Allied Navies and Air Chief Marshal Sir Trafford Leigh-Mallory as C.-in-C. Allied Air Forces. Among those also present were King George VI of England and his first minister, Mr Winston Churchill.

As Reichsfeldmarschall Rommel and his Führer had expected, the Allies' choice of landing site had fallen on the Normandy coast: not only for the fact that the defences there were known to be thinner than in the Pas de Calais area, but because the Cherbourg peninsula was expected to offer some degree of shelter from the Atlantic's worst excesses.

The selected piece of coastline stretched for over forty miles from the base of the Cotentin peninsula to the mouth of the River Orne, west of Cabourg. Following an inland drop by the 82nd and 101st United States Airborne Divisions, the US 4th Infantry Division would land on the most westerly assault beach, code-named "Utah". Fifteen miles to the east, "Omaha" beach was allocated to the US 1st Infantry Division; ten miles further east, at Arromanches, the British 50th Infantry Division, the 8th Armoured Brigade and No. 47 Royal Marine Commando, would go ashore on "Gold", while next to them the Canadian 3rd Infantry Division and 2nd Armoured Brigade were to land on "Juno". On the invasion fleet's left, furthest to the east, "Sword" would be the target for the landing craft of the British 3rd Infantry Division and the 22nd Armoured Brigade, with the 4th Special Service Brigade and Nos 41 and 48 Commandos on their right, and the 1st SS Brigade with No. 4 Commando on their left. The 6th Airborne Division would drop north-east of Caen to protect the eastern flank of the sea-borne landings, and to delay, if not prevent, Rommel's reinforcement of the battle zones.

Further to embarrass the occupying forces, France's secret army was being supplied by air, as witnessed by Jack Crighton in the Forêt d'Othe: since the beginning of May, 80,000 Sten-guns, 30,000 pistols, 17,000 rifles and 3,500 Bren-guns, all with ammunition, had been dropped to the Resistance.

"As the days passed," Crighton would continue, "so the numbers of the Maquis increased. Lots were wanted men - by the Germans, I mean. One day a lad of about fifteen was found snooping around. He was on a forest track used mainly by charcoal burners and he was brought to the camp. He wasn't very forthcoming so they shoved his backside on the fire and he became quite voluble. He had been bribed with cigarettes by the Germans to find the location of the Maquis. They hung him out of hand. I was a bit squeamish about it all so they reminded me that my life too was involved. They said it was a fitting end for a traitor.

Our cook, Jo-Jo, was of Italian origin and as a cook he would have made a good plumber. He used to disappear at night from time to time. I was drinking ersatz coffee and eating brown bread one morning when he returned grinning all over his face. He tossed two objects on the table and grinned even more when he saw my reaction. They were two human ears. Up came my coffee and bread. That was two more collaborators - the Maquis were very hard on those people.

Pierre later showed me a list of hundreds of collaborators in the Province of Aube. Some of the names had been scored off so I assumed they had been dealt with. They found the Sten gun a very handy weapon to the dismay of many who helped the Germans.

About two weeks after they had hung the boy, they picked up two Frenchmen nearby, ostensibly looking to join the Maquis. They were brought to the camp and told to stick around. Pierre told me and the others when we had finished guard duty to watch them and if they tried to escape to shoot them. A few days later, Jo-Jo and a few more took the two away and I noticed they also took shovels. I never saw the two again so I assumed they were well and truly buried. I heard later that friendly Gendarmes had found that they were civil prisoners from Troyes jail working for the Germans on promise of release."

On the eve of D-Day, a gusty wind blew sudden, brief showers across the Normandy beaches, while the moon, having waned and waxed again since it shone so brightly over Mailly-le-Camp, made an occasional appearance through the shifting nimbostratus. It was what a cynical Englishman might have described as a typical June night. A thousand heavy bombers were engaged on operations in support of "Overlord" - attacking coastal defences, knocking down bridges and destroying the railway junctions which lay between the beaches and the enemy reserves. The task of 617 Squadron's Lancaster crews - the one they had rehearsed on the night of 3/4 May, while their commander led the Mosquitos over Mailly-le-Camp - was to convince the enemy that "Overlord" would fall upon the northern coast of France. They were over the North Sea, gradually approaching the coastline of Picardy in a series of overlapping circles at an overall speed of exactly fifteen knots, while the special "window" (or "chaff") they were dropping appeared on German radar screens as the electronic profile of a major naval force.

Meanwhile, a heavy gun battery on the Cotentin peninsular, which commanded the beaches as far east as Le Havre, was the target for a hundred of No. 1 Group's Lancasters. It was from one of these bombers that a rear gunner, the Danish ex-seaman Andreas Moldt, who was known to 166 Squadron as Sergeant Andy Petersen, and whose first operation had been Mailly-le-Camp, looked down from his turret as his pilot, Ivon Warmington, flew home from the target towards the Sussex coast. "In the dark waters,"

Moldt would write, "I could see long, white stripes. I knew from my experience at sea that they were not breaking waves, and so I told the others. Jack looked back from the nose, and he agreed. He said he could see hundreds of ships and, as we came closer to the English coast, I could see more and more. Then came a shout from the bomb-aimer - 'Aircraft with navigation lights on!' They came in small groups of three or four, below us and at different levels. That was when we realised the invasion had begun."

Shortly after midnight, while the 'Overlord' armada was still wallowing and rocking its way across the Channel, a pathfinder force of British paratroopers, the lights of whose aircraft Andy Moldt had seen, silently dropped into the fields between "Sword" beach and Caen. By a series of swift and violent coups de main they prepared a way for the 6th Airborne Division. The task of the division was to establish a bridgehead over the river Orne and the Caen canal for the British and Canadian infantry who, with their armour, would shortly hit the beaches of "Juno" and "Sword". Fifty miles to the west, American paratroops were similarly attempting to isolate the Cotentin Peninsula for the landings on "Utah" and "Omaha" by the US 7th and 5th Corps.

In the grey light of the morning, while the airborne forces were securing their objectives, the Americans on "Utah" were establishing a foothold, but on "Omaha" beach they were pinned down by gunfire and fighting for their lives. In the east, the British and Canadians, aided by tanks and armoured trucks equipped with the "funnies" - the fascines, flails and flame-throwers which the US General Bradley had been offered but had stubbornly declined - were inland of the beaches and thrusting to the south.

While his "Atlantic Wall" was being breached in Normandy, Hitler was deep in a drug-induced sleep, Rommel was far away at General HQ, and von Rundstedt, still believing that the present activity was no more than a feint and that the main threat lay in the Pas de Calais, continued to hold the Panzer divisions in reserve. For this, it would be hard to give him blame: he had little information on which to base a change of plan. He had no air reconnaissance, his communications were fragmented and his radar was either jammed or hoodwinked. Rommel called repeatedly for the 12th SS Panzer and the Panzer Lehr Divisions to be ordered to the beaches, but no such order came - not until Hitler, roused to attend an afternoon conference, recognised the urgency.

When the 6th Airborne landed, General Feuchtinger, commanding the 21st Panzer, on his own initiative, committed a battle group to stem the thrust on Caen. For a while, it looked as though they might succeed. Military historians, analysing the battle, believe that if the 21st had maintained its attack, the paratroopers could have been overwhelmed and the bridgehead restricted. Had the Panzers, pressing on, been able to drive a wedge between the Canadians on "Juno" and the British on "Sword", they might have put Caen out of reach for many a long and bloody day - and Caen was the hinge of the door which Bernard Montgomery meant to open into Europe. For whatever reason, the Panzers withdrew. It may have been the sight of a skyline full of tugs and gliders, escorted by fighters, which discouraged their commanders; it may have been the fact that the British guns had knocked out twenty-six of the ninety tanks they could deploy.

In the Forêt d'Othe, the news of the invasion had not yet filtered through, but the mixed group of Maquisards and evaders knew, by the hubbub of activity among the German troops, that something big was under way.

"It was now evident to Pierre," Crighton would continue, "that the present location was getting too hot and it was time to move. Within two days we moved out to a place that I felt was very vulnerable as it could be surrounded. It was in effect a large copse, probably about three-quarters of a mile long by half a mile wide, separated from the main forest and much nearer to la Lisière-des-Bois.

Still more members arrived, and also a new chief, or Commandant as the French called him. After Pierre, who looked the part, I didn't go much on the new chief. He looked more like a gentleman farmer. He even brought his own tent. After he had been with us a few days, we stopped a car and captured three known collaborators - two men and a very smart woman. They shot the men but the new chief found a use for the woman in his tent.

Meanwhile I had an attack of boils on my back. I think it was the food or the lack of it. Between that and the shortage of cigarettes we all got a bit edgy at times. The news of the 'débarquement' - the invasion - on the 6th June, however, cheered us all no end. The Maquis boys went crazy and strutted around locally armed to the teeth.

After this foolishness the inevitable happened and Jerry and the White Russians arrived with heavy machine guns and mortars. There were about 2,000 of them. The French boys knocked out a few of the trucks with troops aboard, but once Jerry got his mortars going things got very uncomfortable. Even in the woods, the crump of mortars overhead was very unpleasant. This went on for hours until we ran out of ammunition. I did hear one Bren going long after the rest of us had run out. I found myself with six Frenchmen at the other end of the copse overlooking a field. Two of them made a break but they didn't get twenty yards before they were shot down. The others and I looked for the thickest cover and decided to wait for nightfall. It was about eight o'clock and time was really dragging. One of the Frenchmen pulled out a grenade and asked us to form a small circle. He said if the Boche came he'd pull the pin and we'd all go together. He said Jerry would torture us first and then shoot us. This way we would escape torture. Life to me at that moment was very sweet and I prayed that Jerry would stay away.

That night as darkness fell we crept down towards the village where we eventually met up with Pierre. He thought about thirty of the Maquis had died. I asked him about Bert Townsend but he didn't know. He said there was a big Maquis down south but I said I'd had a bellyful of the Maquis. We laid low all night and Pierre said he'd sort out something in the morning."

Although he didn't say so, the Maquis leader believed that the air-gunner had been killed in the battle. Indeed, there is a grave at la Lisière-des-Bois with Townsend's name on the headstone. The grave, however, contains the remains of another airman, who was similarly dressed when he died in the forest.

"About midday, Pierre came to our hiding place and called me. We went down the road to where I was introduced to an insignificant-looking little man. This was M. Joseph Lebrun, but I found out later that although he was small he was far from insignificant. He had a car like no car I'd seen before. It had a boiler mounted on the back which burned wood. I discovered it was the only civilian car in Estissac. Joe was the Poste Auto Rurale - in other words, the postman for all the district and farms around Estissac.

I bade Pierre goodbye and set off with Joe. We travelled about sixteen kilometres, taking quiet country roads. Joe kept smiling and reassuring me that all would be well. We eventually came to a town which Joe said was Estissac. A few minutes later we pulled into the front yard of a house and Joe indicated that this was journey's end. As we entered the house we were welcomed by five little girls, the eldest about thirteen years old, and a large lady who was Madame Lebrun.

Joe then took me upstairs and, pulling aside a wardrobe,

opened a door. Behind it were two of my crew - Flying Officer
Maurice Garlick and Flight Sergeant Paddy O'Hara. I don't know
who was most surprised. When Joe understood, he was delighted."

The three evaders of Q-Queenie's crew stayed with Lebrun while the
Maquis licked its wounds. Garlick's legs healed, thanks to Lebrun's skilful
treatment, and he was fit to move about, albeit on sticks. O'Hara and Crighton
were eager for action. The Allies had established a foothold, and were fighting
their way inland from the beaches. The word from London was that the
Maquisards, working in small, local groups, should make themselves as much
of a nuisance to the Germans as they could, disrupting lines of communication,
harassing movement and keeping note of dispositions. Crighton would
describe what was happening in Estissac:

"With the children around there was never a dull moment.
They never mentioned us outside, for that would have been fatal.
Every morning Joe would go through his ritual, starting up his
wood-burning car and plugging into the mains to save the
battery. We used to stand by and listen. All you could hear was
"merde, merde, merde" - which is a rude word in French. One of
my daily chores was chopping firewood for stoking Joe's car. His
mobility was invaluable to the resistance. The things carried in
that car ranged from Sten guns, grenades and plastic explosives
to farm produce. He once picked up some German officers
whose car had broken down when he had a milk churn full of
Sten guns on board.

A market gardener living nearby was hiding a Flight
Lieutenant and two American Fortress boys. The Flight
Lieutenant was shot down in a Mosquito at Mailly. He was a
Scotty from Prestwick near my own home in Ayrshire. Joe took
Paddy and me to the local cinema one night and when we heard
German voices behind us we were as quiet as church mice, but
the old market gardener's boys rode bicycles in the streets of
Estissac in broad daylight.

One day our bedroom door opened and a gendarme walked
in. He frightened the daylights out of us, but he was a friend, and
kept Joe informed of German movements. Apparently there was
a lot of German activity around, so Paddy and I went off to the
woods until things cooled down again. During the time we were
there we caught sight of the wild pigs or 'les sangliers' as the
French called them. They looked really nasty hairy devils. A

Frenchman told me that if you shot one and only wounded it, your best bet was the nearest tree. When I saw the holes they dug looking for truffles, I could well believe their tusks were lethal.

When the heat was off we went back to Joe's. Madame Lebrun was very frightened and with five children she had every right to be. Paddy and I thought it best to try and make our way to Switzerland but Joe said that if we were caught it would be more dangerous still. He reckoned the Boche had ways of making people talk.

Three Frenchmen arrived at the house. Two of them were saboteurs who were being introduced to Joe by the third man. When they found I had been with the Maquis they became very friendly. I found myself making up plastic bombs on Joe's kitchen table when the children had gone to bed. All they had to do then was to stick them on a suitable section of railway line and set the timing device. The object of the exercise was to leave trains and rolling stock out in the open where Allied fighters would see them and have a good time. The Germans would never move railway traffic by daylight because they were sitting ducks for the fighters. I often saw Lightnings over Estissac looking for German transport.

We heard rumours of an American armoured Division getting near the town of Sens and Joe decided to go and look for them. He came back all hot and bothered a short time later. He had mounted American and British flags on the front of his car and the Germans took a dim view of that. Luckily he got away before any bullets hit his car."

Two days later, Lebrun made another sortie in his remarkable vehicle. This time, he took his lodgers with him, and all were armed with Sten guns. They found the US Army at Auxerre, forty miles south-south-west of Estissac in the province of Yonne. The Colonel in command, having plied his visitors with cigarettes and candy, took note of what Lebrun, as interpreted by Garlick, could tell him about the Wehrmacht dispositions, and promised that Estissac would be free within a matter of days. It was, indeed, from that area that he proposed to mount an offensive against the garrison at Troyes.

Sure enough, on the 22nd August, three Sherman tanks rolled into Estissac, and the news of their coming spread through the village like fire through a haystack. Monsieur Mary Rilliot, now the deputy mayor, and then a young farmer, remembers their arrival as though it happened yesterday. "The

Greg Biefer (2nd from the left) with another radar mechanic (1st left), and four of the crew of 12 Sqn's S-Sugar: Pilot Officer Pollard from Trinidad (Captain), Sergeant Reneau (Wireless Op), Sergeant Alberry (Flight Engineer) and Flight Sergeant Wettlaufer, RCAF (Navigator). The crew took part in the attack; the aircraft with Pollard and Wettlaufer were lost on 30 June/1 July.

tanks were going around with flags, everyone was excited. We thought it was the liberation! But my father, who had known the first war, said we shouldn't be too hasty - it wasn't over yet. He was right. The tanks went away. Next day, the Germans came back. In the meantime, some young men had taken the German flag down from the bell-tower of the church and replaced it with the tricolour. The Germans found the culprits - all five. You must understand that there were always those who were ready to denounce the patriots. There were Nazi sympathisers - whole families of them. Some are still here today. Of course, when the Resistance discovered the informers..."

It was another three days before the village of Estissac was truly liberated. Then, the tanks, the trucks, the jeeps and the men of the US 4th Division arrived in force, but they came just too late for those five young patriots, whose lives, for "terrorist activities", were the last things Hitler's soldiers took before they left.

The "Front Français de l'Intérieur", the "Front Tireurs Patriote", the Maquisards and the men of the Resistance were agreed on this, if not on all other matters: the victims' bodies should be buried with military honours. Garlick, Crighton and O'Hara were invited to represent the Royal Air Force. Garlick looked at his companions, and they at him. He approached the Colonel's temporary headquarters. "These chaps were fighting the enemy," he said, "just the same as us. We can't go to their funeral dressed like this. Could you possibly..."

"Sure I can, son," said the Colonel, and arrayed the airmen in good GI uniforms. That last, sad occasion past, the villagers allowed themselves to celebrate. Enthusiastically, if still a little prematurely, the Maquis threw a Victory party, at which the RAF and USAAF evaders were the guests of honour. Next day, the village was en fête. The fine wines and spirits (the 'quality stuff', was Crighton's description), which had lain hidden in cellars and hay-lofts for four years of occupation, were lavishly dispensed. One of the Colonel's officers, given a glass of calvados - the local apple brandy - downed it at a gulp, and lost the power of speech for half an hour.

The US Army moved on towards Troyes, leaving a Jeep and a driver to help the evaders on their way back to England. They had spent three months with Joseph Lebrun, postman extraordinary - three months of sharing food and danger, and nothing can form a closer bond. Their farewells were said with some emotion. "Joe was in tears," Crighton would remember, "and the children too. We had become a part of the Lebrun family."

Of the 192 Squadron crew, Stormont and Munro remained under cover until the Liberation in the area of Polisot, on the river Seine between Troyes and Dijon, where, in early June, they had hidden from the Germans beneath the floorboards of a château. Ackroyd and Preece suffered beatings and starvation in different civil gaols before the Gestapo, at last convinced that they had nothing to impart, handed them over to the Abwehr as prisoners of war. They were then to be penned in a succession of Stalags, each further eastward than the last, until, in Poland, exactly a year since the night when they had baled out of the Halifax, the advancing Russian Armies set them free.

Sergeant Preece.

The evaders from Estissac spent three days in newly-liberated Paris before flying home to England early in September. The rear gunner, Bert Townsend, who, after the battle at la Lisière-des-Bois, had joined a sabotage group, returned by sea. Q-Queenie's pilot, Peter Maxwell, by his own devices, had made his way back to England a month before his crew (as had Harry Gibson, the pilot of the Halifax) and was already flying again - as an instructor. None of the evaders returned to operations: they knew too much about the French Resistance to be allowed to fall into the hands of the Gestapo.

Sergeant Stormont.

In London, Garlick, Crighton and O'Hara were well scrubbed (it had been noticeable on the Hendon-bound Dakota that other passengers had kept a careful distance), deloused and daubed with a solution of potassium permanganate. At an Air Ministry establishment, they were subjected to interrogation - no whips or rubber truncheons, only friendly faces and cups of hot, sweet tea. While, however, Crighton told his story, his Maquis rifle and his bagful of the "quality stuff" disappeared from the waiting room. "Four months with the Resistance," he muttered, "and what have I got? A third of an op in my log book!"

CHAPTER TEN

THE ANALYSIS

When the de-briefing reports from the squadrons had been analysed, the general feeling in the higher reaches of command was that the purpose of the raid had been achieved, and this impression was confirmed by the evidence brought back from the target on Friday, 6th May by a reconnoitring Spitfire of No. 541 Squadron. The highly-skilled photographic interpreters, having carried out their examination of twin prints in stereo, made their assessment:

"Although practically the whole of the target has been severely damaged, the main weight of the attack has fallen on the large compact group of MT and barrack buildings. Out of 47 MT buildings at the north side of the site not one has escaped damage, 34 being totally destroyed. A larger group of about 114 barrack buildings have also suffered very severely, 47 being destroyed and many of the remainder damaged.

The workshops to the south of this group are more dispersed and lie outside the greatest concentration of craters, many have nevertheless been destroyed and scarcely any has escaped damage. A second group of MT buildings to the east has suffered similarly. Further to the east of the built-up area, the ammunition dump and the range have both been hit.

The main concentration of craters which blankets the
barrack and MT buildings extends into the open ground to the
north. Several craters are visible in the training area and in the
vicinity of tank garages to the east."

The compilers of the report then went on to identify the damaged
buildings, singly or in groups, by reference to numbers stencilled on the prints.
The PR pilot had taken his photographs in mid-afternoon, and even a layman
could tell, by the shadows on the ground among the rows of buildings, which
were still standing and which had been knocked down. Gaping holes could be
seen in other structures, including the water-tower. The whole centre of the
photograph, showing the built-up area, appeared to be speckled with hundreds
of black dots, which were in fact craters made by the "cookies". There was
some evidence of "creep-back", but the great majority of the bombs falling
short had dropped in open fields.

The assessment was summarised at High Wycombe and passed down,
through both Group Headquarters, to the bomber squadrons. There, although
some bitterness remained about the deadly hiatus (and does so to this day
among a number of veterans, some of whom - mistakenly - blame Leonard
Cheshire for being too "pernickety" about the early marking), the feeling of
accomplishment also percolated down - especially to those squadrons whose
losses had been light. No. 463 Squadron of 5 Group, for example, had
despatched twelve aircraft of which eleven had returned, each, according to
the Intelligence Officer at Waddington, with an aiming-point photograph,
and the officer responsible for compiling the Squadron's Form 540, in
recording this achievement, did not attempt to hide a certain savage
satisfaction: "Our squadron went into the attack with zeal," he wrote,
"knowing we were going to kill a few thousand German soldiers with their
staff officers billeted at the camp - mainly tank divisions. Photos reveal great
devastation which must have killed some thousands of Germans trained to
top pitch for meeting our invasion force."

Subsequently, a report by the Wehrmacht officer commanding the depot
came into the hands of the staff at High Wycombe; while it did not entirely
support the conclusions of the enthusiastic officer at Waddington, it was not
unimpressive - certainly not as to the structural damage. In translation, the
report read as follows: "The main concentration was accurately aimed at the
most important buildings. In that part of the camp which was destroyed, the
concentration was so great that not only did the splinter-proof shelters receive
direct hits, but even the bombs which missed choked them up and made the
sides cave in. Additional casualties were caused because soldiers used a short

break in the bombing to recover their weapons and gear, and were caught in a fresh hail of bombs."

When the water-tower was hit, it was revealed, the ensuing deluge had flooded a nearby trench, and drowned a number of soldiers whose ill luck it had been to be taking shelter there. The loss of water had also inhibited the fire-fighting effort, and the fire brigade from Troyes had been summoned to assist. The fuel dump fire, which was probably the fiercest, had engulfed a group of soldiers whose refuge was close by.

The total casualties in the camp, as recorded in the German archives, were 218 killed or missing and 156 wounded; of these, a high proportion were non-commissioned officers. 102 vehicles were destroyed, including 37 tanks. Of the buildings - the barracks, messes, workshops and offices - 80% were destroyed, and the other 20% were damaged, although worthy of repair.

There can be no doubt that the first delay - after the Oboe flares and Cheshire's red spot fires had gone down, and before the heavies' bombs began to fall - gave the Panzertruppen time to take shelter and saved many of their lives. The second hiatus, when the onslaught was sporadic and some men left the trenches to fetch their equipment or to fight the fires, fortuitously cost the troops a number of casualties, although not so many as it cost the RAF. It was the final attack, largely concentrated between 0026 and 0034 hours, when the bombers in the orbit were at last unleashed, which brought the heaviest destruction - so heavy that it caused a veteran Feldwebel to mutter, as he supervised the transport of bodies for burial in Troyes, "It was like Cologne - horrible!". The unremitting hail of high explosive so unmanned some survivors that next morning, as they emerged from the woods where they had cowered all night, they were observed by witnesses to be holding their hands up and constantly crying "Kamerad!"

It had always been a fear of Winston Churchill's that such attacks as this would cost France dearly in civilian lives. Remarkably, in this instance, very few were lost. There were ten deaths in Poivres, two miles north-east of the target, and six houses damaged, some by shot-down Lancasters, some by undershooting bombs. In Trouans, two-and-a-half miles to the south, the bodies of a family of four were buried alongside the hastily-dug graves of the men whose falling aircraft had destroyed their home.

Recording the enemy defences, a section of the "Bomber Command Report on Night Operations", classified "Secret", read as follows:

"ENEMY DEFENCES

9. Ground defences. 8 heavy guns were in action at the target, firing accurately at 8-9,000 feet. Light flak came from 20

Four views of Mailly-le-Camp, a few days after the raid.

guns, and was self-destroying at 10-12,000 feet. Only 3 searchlights exposed in the moonlight. Accurate flak was met en route from airfields and Chartres.

10. Fighters. The first interceptions occurred on the SE leg beyond Compiègne, and at first the enemy lost more heavily than did the bombers, losing 3, probably 4, fighters before we turned S near Epernay. Then the unfortunate delay before the aircraft received their instructions resulted in a concentration of aircraft over the datum point in bright moonlight, presenting fighters with great opportunities of wholesale interceptions. The attack lasted 19 minutes longer than had been planned, and it was during this period that most of the losses occurred. Fighters were active over the whole of the westerly route home, until the coast was reached.

ENEMY AIRCRAFT DESTROYED

11. Our bombers destroyed 4, probably 6, aircraft: one Me 109, two Me 110s and a FW 190 for certain, with a Ju 88 and an unidentified twin-engined fighter as probables.

CASUALTIES

12. 42 aircraft (11.3%) were lost - a very high percentage, especially for a French target. The main reason has been given above - the concentration at the datum point because of the delay in instructing the main force. At least 25 aircraft fell in combat, rather more than half of those over the target, and all the rest on the homeward run. 9 were lost to flak, mostly over the target, although the defences of Romilly, Fontainebleau and Chartres claimed victims. The other 8 losses cannot definitely be placed. 2 returning aircraft were wrecked by fighter attack."

The two wrecked Lancasters referred to in the report's last sentence were 550 Squadron's BQ J-Jig, which was crash-landed at Ford, and 576 Squadron's UL S-Sugar Two, in which the crew struggled back to Elsham Wolds with a dead rear gunner on board. Both aircraft were so badly damaged that they had to be written off charge.

The loss-rate of 11.3% quoted earlier in the paragraph was presumably a miscalculation. The figure should have been 11.6% - 42 lost out of 362 despatched, as recorded in the "Bomber Command Intelligence Narrative of Operations". In this document, also classified "Secret", which was distributed to all units at 2350 hours on 4 May, the statistics were as follows:

Gp	Type	Despat-ched	Succ-essful	Abort-ive	Missing	Tons dropped HE	Tis
1	Lancaster	173	138	7	28	722.5	0.3
5	Lancaster	173	158	1	14	762.9	8.0
5	Mosquito	14	12	1		4.5	0.4
8	Mosquito	2	2				0.9

Included in the 1 Group figures are those for the small force dedicated to the "special target". Twenty-nine Lancasters from Nos. 460 and 625 Squadrons and four from the Special Duty Flight took off on this assignment; twelve of the bombers and three of the markers attacked their primary objective, nine bombers were diverted to the main depot target, and six, including the one from the SD Flight, were shot down. Two of the bombers and one of the markers had abortive sorties, the former "NOET" (not over enemy territory), and the latter "OET" (over enemy territory).

All the 1 Group Lancasters, except those of the SD Flight, whose loads included a 250-pound green spot fire, carried a 4000-pound "cookie" and sixteen 500-pound, medium-case bombs. Most 5 Group Lancasters took similar loads, but the two marker squadrons, Nos. 83 and 97, carried spot fires and flares as well as HE bombs, and seventeen other aircraft carried four one-thousand pounders instead of a 'cookie'.

As to the Luftwaffe's activities, it is clear that every night-fighter crew with a serviceable aircraft, based on an airfield within range of the bombers' route, was airborne at some time during the attack: several, indeed, made more than one sortie. Less than half the force, however - some twenty-five crews - were engaged in combat, and of these twenty-two reported one or more successes, amounting to a total of fifty-one claims. The losses recorded by Bomber Command, including those of the squadrons engaged on subsidiary operations, were exactly that. Although Dr. Göbbels might well enhance them later, Nachtjagdgeschwader claims were usually accurate; even if two night-fighter pilots, both having fired upon the same bomber, each claimed a kill, so thorough were the German methods of cross-checking with sightings on the ground that duplicated claims were normally ruled out. (Under the Luftwaffe system, Fighter Command's initial claim of 183 aircraft destroyed on 15 September 1940, at the height of the Battle of Britain, would have been coldly whittled down to the more realistic figure of 60.)

The German champions of the night, both flying Bf-110s, were

Hauptmann Helmut Bergmann, flying from Juvincourt, who claimed six "shoot-downs", and Hauptmann Martin Drewes, the Kommandeur of III Gruppe NJG 1, based at Athies-sur-Laon, who claimed five - all in the course of a flight which lasted forty minutes. Drewes and his radar man, Unteroffizier Handke, found their first Lancaster over the target, and shot it down eight miles to the south; their last victim was 44 Squadron's KM K-King, which went down fifty miles west of Paris on the homeward route - her crew were probably the last to die that night.

Three Bf-110s fell to the guns of the Lancasters: two from I Gruppe NJG 4, based at Florennes, and one from III Gruppe NJG 4 at Laon. The first, with Feldwebel Kraft and his crew, went down near Juvincourt, on the bombers' outbound route; the second, flown by Leutnant Duttmann, crashed at Vitry-le-François, eleven miles east of the target; the third, with Leutnant Helm at the controls, hit the ground at Lardy, twenty-five miles south of Paris. Since the Lancaster gunners only claimed two aircraft of this type, it is probable that the fighter originally claimed by Sergeant Garlick of 12 Squadron as an He-111 (an identification which he later came to doubt), was actually Leutnant Helm's Bf-110. The skills of air gunners in aircraft recognition, however carefully studied in the classroom, sometimes failed to stand up to the harsh examination of actual experience. When a night-fighter suddenly appeared out of the darkness with guns and cannon blazing, the question as to whether it had been constructed by Heinkel, Messerschmitt or Junkers was, for the moment, purely academic.

There was a noticeable contrast between the views of the Mailly-le-Camp attack taken by the aircrews in the first wave, who were largely from 5 Group, and those of the 1 Group crews who followed them. Hank Harpham of 5 Group's 83 Squadron, for example, when asked about the timing and the way the raid progressed, was clear in his opinion. "There was no delay," he stated, "and our time on target was as briefed. We encountered some flak, but we weren't hit, and we saw no enemy fighters. We heard no unusual RT chatter over the target. As far as we were concerned, there was no free-for-all." Louis Wayte of 1 Group's 166 Squadron, on the other hand, said "We were kept waiting, and the fighters had a birthday. Then it was a free-for-all."

As to their experiences over the assembly-point, reports by the 1 Group crews, although differing in detail, were essentially the same. "The most memorable part of the whole operation," said George Wilson of 626 Squadron, "was when we were circling that ground marker, tethered like live bait, watching aircraft explode in the air and on the ground. Voices on the RT began to show signs of strain. Most of the noise came from an Aussie, and his irritation was very infectious. More people gave vent to their feelings, then one of the marker pilots broke in. I can't remember exactly what he said, because his words came out in such a spate, but he indicated that we would all have to wait, because he was being chased all over the sky. That quietened most of them, but two or three went on, abrasive and monotonous as rooks, until a voice I recognised said 'You undisciplined lot of bastards, shut up!' The Aussie made an impolite rejoinder, then he faded out, too. The silence was a great relief: apart from the effect on the nerves of all those nagging voices, they interfered with concentration, and we were trying to concentrate on looking out for fighters. In fact, I suppose there were never more than ten voices on the air, and you have to remember that there were several hundred aircraft in the orbit, but it did seem at one time that the air was filled with voices, on the brink of panic."

Stewart Black's navigator in PH C-Charlie, Warrant Officer Roy Holding, a twenty-year old from Welwyn in Saskatchewan, made a similar comment: "There was a lot of chatter, very crude and uncomplimentary, especially one 'down-under' voice who used a lot of four-letter words. Of course, we were all used to the language, and used it in our daily conversation, but somehow it seemed out of place on the radio, over enemy territory. Probably a lot of it was prompted by frustration and fear, but it was a poor show - regardless of our having to wait."

Squadron Leader Shannon's navigator, Len Sumpter, who was well-acquainted with 5 Group's low-level marking technique, when asked what he thought about the impatience demonstrated by some captains on the RT, gave this reply: "It showed they weren't used to concentrated bombing on small targets. They were used to getting in and out as soon as possible, like on a Big City raid. It was different in 617. I remember when we went to the Bielefeld Viaduct in daylight, we were milling around for ages waiting for our turn to bomb."

There was general agreement at all levels of command that the heavy casualties over the assembly-point were due to a failure in communications between the crews and the Controller. What the contemporary reports do not reveal is the widespread unawareness of the plan in its entirety. One example, already briefly mentioned, is startling enough to merit further airing.

The 1 Group Operation Order, while stating that the main attack on the east and west ends of the depot would be under the command of the "5 Group Controller", required that the marking and bombing of the "special target" should be directed by the "1 Group Controller". Only the crews immediately concerned, however - the Special Duty Flight markers and the

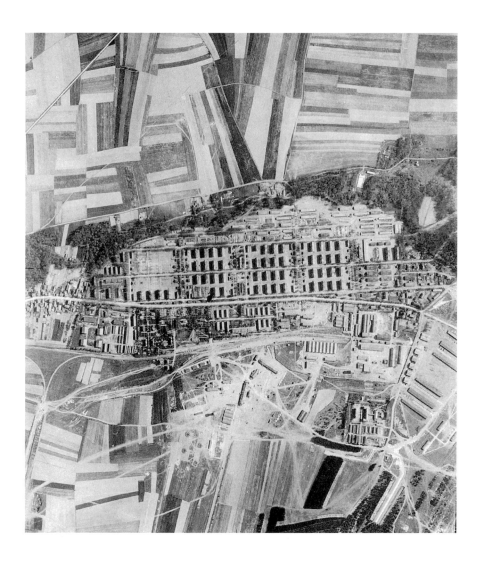

Photo Reconnaissance picture taken before the raid, April 23, 1994.

Photo Reconnaissance picture taken after the raid, May 6, 1994.

twenty-nine selected crews from Binbrook and Kelstern - appear to have
known of that arrangement; none of the other 1 Group pilots questioned
remembered having heard of it. Furthermore, Wing Commander (later Group
Captain) Laurence Deane, DSO, DFC, who was the OC No. 83 Squadron and
the officer appointed by No. 5 Group as the Main Force Controller, was quite
clear about the matter: "My role was the sole Controller of the raid," he
informed your author. "No. 1 Group were part of the main force and had no
Controller of their own."

A brief survey of the other operations undertaken on the night of 3rd/4th
May may serve to set the main attack in context. Twenty-seven Mosquitoes of
8 Group's Light Night Striking Force accurately bombed Ludwigshaven, and
another nine destroyed the ammunition dump at Châteaudun, where an initial
vast explosion was followed by a series of lesser ones which were seen to last
for half-an-hour.

The "gardening" force of thirty-two Halifaxes from Nos. 4 and 6 Groups
laid sixty-two mines in enemy waters, and the thirty-four OTU Wellingtons
and Whitleys completed their "nickeling" missions. No aircraft were lost or
damaged on any of these missions.

A mixed bag of 3 Group aircraft - twenty-three altogether - completed
their clandestine activities with the loss to No. 161 Squadron of a Westland
Lysander (a sturdy, single-engined, high-winged monoplane, which could take
off and land in a football field, and was much used for the delivery and
collection of secret agents).

Three Halifaxes of No. 100 Group's 192 Squadron flew RCM sorties,
and one of their number, as has been recorded, was shot down near the target.
In all, during May, the squadron undertook eighty-one sorties, from which
only DT V-Victor and one other aircraft failed to return. Without the efforts of
these specialist crews to disrupt control and communications, the main force
losses might have been yet heavier, not only on the night of 3/4 May, but on
subsequent attacks. Of ten 100 Group Mosquito II crews on intruder patrols,
none found a target to engage - not even the five over Mailly-le-Camp; one
crew, however, from 169 Squadron, based at Little Snoring, themselves
became a target, and were shot down near the depot. (It was a member of this
crew, nonchalantly riding a cycle down the main street of Estissac, whom
Jack Crighton of 12 Squadron's Q-Queenie was to encounter two months
later.) There should have been twelve of these 100 Group intruders, but two
returned early, having been "unable to establish their position over enemy
territory" - a kinder way of saying that they were lost. In fairness to the
intruder crews it has to be recorded, not only that the AI Mark IV set did not

function well in tandem with the "Serrate" homer, but that any navigator over five feet tall had the utmost difficulty in using the "Gee" box, so awkward was its position in the cockpit.

The twelve light bomber Mosquitos of 2 Group attacked enemy installations in France, as had been planned, and the eight ADGB fighter Mosquitos, incurring no losses and finding no victims, carried out what were described as successful patrols over enemy airfields.

The major subsidiary effort was the attack made by eighty-four Lancasters and eight Oboe Mosquitos of No. 8 Group on the Luftwaffe base at Montdidier, and although the crews of four Mosquitos and four Lancasters had various sorts of technical trouble which caused them to abort, the remainder were sufficient to mark and bomb the target. Three hundred and seventy-eight tons of HE bombs were dropped; four Lancasters were lost - one each from Nos. 35 and 405 Squadrons, and two from 582 Squadron - a loss-rate of exactly five per cent. The attack, as assessed at High Wycombe, was entirely successful.

In comparing the loss-rate at Montdidier with that at Mailly-le-Camp, where over 12% of the Lancasters were lost, the differences between the two operations must be taken into account. Clearly, the shorter range of the Montdidier mission - 150 miles there and back as compared with 320 miles for Mailly-le-Camp - meant less than half the period at risk. Also, the aircraft and equipment stores at Montdidier offered a slightly less demanding target: the tank depot's buildings were concentrated in a smaller area and closer to a village. But the principal difference between the two operations lay in the nature of their tactical plans, which compared with one another in their complexity as the riddle of the Sphinx with a Christmas-cracker puzzle. For Mailly-le-Camp, the plan had to accommodate three separate aiming-points, with different sets of spot fires following the Oboe markers at overlapping times. For Montdidier, after similar initial marking, red and green spot fires were dropped by the Mosquitos and corrected, as necessary, by the Master Bomber, who then called in a single wave of heavy bombers. (The advantage of using markers of two colours was that the Master Bomber could pick the more accurate and direct the Lancasters accordingly.) There was, furthermore, this crucial distinction: over Montdidier one RT channel was in use throughout.

The facts, then, of the Mailly-le-Camp operation, or most of them, are known - the logistics, the tactics, the achievement and the cost. As to the logistics, there is room for debate as to whether they were sound. It has already been argued that the weight of the attack was disproportionate to the dimensions of the depot, and here another comment by Len Sumpter, the experienced 617 Squadron navigator, is pertinent: "There was an element of overkill - such a large force on such a small target."

The selection of the bomb-load must also be questioned. The 4,000 pound "cookies" were designed for city targets - for knocking down office-blocks and factories, blocking roads and railway lines, fracturing gas-pipes and sewage systems - but smaller bombs, 1,000 or 500 pounders, might have been more effective against the depot buildings and the personnel (and would certainly have been a lesser threat to the low-flying marker crews of 617 Squadron). There was, after all, no question of aiming at individual tanks or armoured vehicles: any direct hit on either was bound to be fortuitous. 617 Squadron's spot fires were aimed at the east and west ends of the depot buildings, and the Lancasters' bomb-loads were, in turn, dropped on the spot fires. The fact that, within these parameters, accuracy was sought - hence the selection of the bombing altitude and choice of a moonlit night for the attack - is another reason for believing that the "cookie", which was shaped like a domestic hot-water cylinder and had ballistic characteristics to match, may not have been the right bomb for the job.

Whether the tactics, the *modi operandi*, were ill-conceived or not must be a matter of opinion; of the fact that they failed there can be no dispute. The novel ingredients - the allocation of aiming-points between two bomber groups, and the attempt to synchronise the marking of three separate attacks - were always likely to prove incompatible with tactical success.

From Leonard Cheshire's evidence, it is clear that the target information and the requirement reached him late in the morning of the 3rd May. There was no time for framing new tactics to suit the operation. The best he could do was to adapt those that had proved effective, and had been accepted, as the 5 Group method of attacking small targets. As Cheshire recognised, they rested largely on communications, and it is probably true that, given reliable air-to-air radio, and a fool-proof system which was understood by all, the tactics might have prospered, despite their complexity. Even the general unawareness among the bomber captains of exactly what was planned might not have been a major problem if the communications had been good. The attack might yet have succeeded in destroying the depot without a sickening death-roll among the bomber crews if there had been a fall-back plan - a line of action to follow if the system failed, but there was none. The communications plan was inadequate, tactically and technically, and there was no official fall-back - only what could be improvised on the spur of the moment, among the flares and the moonlight and the burning Lancasters.

As Laurence Deane was to write in his subsequent account: "The results could be said to justify the high loss, but how much more satisfactory it would have been if the instructions to bomb had been received with no delay."

The reasons for the failure in communications were examined at the time, but only superficially, and not entirely satisfactorily: there was, after all, a war going on. The truth of all that happened on the radio, high above the target, after the first set of Oboe markers fell, may never be revealed. The following assessment, although based on fact, inevitably and admittedly includes an element of guesswork.

The Marker Leader had a VHF frequency in common with his Mosquito crews, and another with Cochrane's PFF and the Main Force Controller. Technically, there was never any problem with their communications, although there were misunderstandings. The main force captains did not share that frequency: they expected to hear the Controller's instructions on their VHF channel "C" (channel "A" was always tuned to their own base frequency, "D" was for distress calls, and "B" was used for bombing ranges or other special purposes). The Controller's impression was that, unlike the 5 Group Lancasters, those of 1 Group were not equipped with VHF. This was not the case, but it is what he recalls from the way that he was briefed, and here it must be said that, from his understanding of it, the Controller's briefing at Coningsby, one way or another, was inadequate, if not to say inaccurate, and not only in the matter - the really vital matter - of the radio facilities: he was, as he recalls, entirely unaware of the two separate aiming-points on the main depot site and of the 1 Group "special target". Compared with these deficiencies, his unawareness of the fact that all but a handful of the Lancasters carried 4,000 pounders - which led to his bumpy flight across the target - dims into insignificance.

In the same context, it was not only Laurence Deane who heard "duff gen" at briefing. Dave Kearns of 617 Squadron was surprised when your author informed him that the heavies' bombing height as detailed was between six and eight thousand feet, and that many dropped their bombs from lower altitudes than that. "As far as I can recall," he responded, "the only aircraft below 10,000 over the target area were to be our four Mosquitos."

Under the impression, then, that the 1 Group aircraft had no VHF, the Controller believed that his instructions to the aircraft of both groups had to be passed by his wireless operator, using the Morse code, on the command WT frequency. The trouble was that none of the main force wireless operators knew anything of this. Those with "Fishpond" were watching their radar screens; those not so equipped were, at that stage of the mission, probably in the astro-dome, making an extra pair of eyes to search the sky for fighters. It must be reiterated, furthermore, that even if they had been briefed to listen out for messages from the Controller, they would only have heard them if their receivers had been as far off frequency as was his transmitter.

After Leonard Cheshire had dropped his red spot fires, thirty seconds after midnight, five minutes passed, for one reason or another, before Shannon's markers followed. The delay was long enough to worry Laurence Deane, but not long enough to impress itself on the memory of the 5 Group crews who bombed during that phase of the operation. Two or three captains, awaiting no instructions, went in to bomb as soon as they saw Shannon's spot fires on the ground. Others followed them. Some heard the order "Bomb" on VHF, but whether from the Controller, who may by then have resorted to that medium (although, admittedly, he does not remember doing so), or from his deputy, who had summed up what was happening and was doing his best to help, cannot be determined, and it does not really matter very much. The fact is that only approximately a third of the 5 Group force, and a few impatient 1 Group crews, had bombed the eastern aiming point by 0015 hours - three minutes later than the time by which, according to the plan, the entire first attack-wave of a hundred and seventy-three Lancasters, having bombed the target, should have been on their way home.

Then came the second, and more serious, hiatus. It began with a misunderstanding between the Marker Leader and the Controller. Cheshire knew that the "re-marking" (as he thought of it) of the second, western aiming-point, by Kearns and Fawke was overdue, and he wanted the bombing to stop while they undertook their task. Deane, unaware of any second aiming point, thought Cheshire meant a reinforcement of the existing spot fires on the initial aiming-point, which could readily be carried out by one or more of the "Backers-up", as was standard PFF practice, with no halt in the bombing. Deane, therefore, seeing no need to stop, did not pass the order on. Sparks, however, either knowing or divining what the Marker Leader wanted, sharply and repeatedly told the second wave to wait.

Not every pilot heard him, not every pilot heeded him (as Cheshire would recount "the bombing never ceased"), but by far the majority of the 1 Group crews, and many of 5 Group's, continued to orbit that dire assembly-point. By the time Kearns and Fawke had dropped the second batch of spot fires, the 5 Group aircraft should have been nineteen minutes' worth of air miles on the route for home, and the 1 Group attack was four minutes overdue. Such a delay, by no means remarkable in 617 Squadron's experience, might not have been disastrous, if the 1 Group Lancasters' arrival at the assembly-point had been ten minutes later than it was. Those ten minutes may have cost the Command a hundred lives.

Leonard Cheshire, looking back across the years, made this comment:

"Basically, we did not like having to mark a target to be bombed by the Main Force, simply because our system of doing this depended upon a fairly sophisticated and well worked out tactical plan, which depended heavily upon good communications. To bring in crews who had never heard of the technique and were not used to constant RT (or WT) communications during the raid was, in our opinion, putting both them and us at a disadvantage. Of course, where it was a question of area bombing, such as at Munich a week or so previously, this would not matter so much. But Mailly put us in exactly the invidious, and potentially dangerous, situation we had envisaged. This, moreover, was compounded by two factors: (1) lack of time for proper preparation and consultation due to the late receipt of orders: (2) the refusal to allow 617's Lancasters to participate. Had even some of them been up there I think we could have solved the communication problems." (Cheshire's Lancasters, as has been reported, were engaged on a rehearsal of their D-Day operation, flying in overlapping circles off the coast of Norfolk while a group of technicians with a captured German radar tried - and failed - to identify them through the clouds of "window".)

Then, remembering his attempts to halt the operation at the height of the battle over the assembly-point, and to send the waiting bombers home, Cheshire had this afterthought: "All the same, it may be I was mistaken in my judgement and that inflicting the maximum possible damage on the barracks could have played a crucial role when it came to the invasion a month later."

In that corollary, Cheshire illustrates the inevitable dilemma of the commander: is the game worth the candle? Will the operation's outcome justify the losses? Among the "ifs" to be pondered about the D-Day action - and there are many, as there are and always will be about the conduct of great battles - there are grounds for believing that, if the 21st Panzer Division had been at full strength, if it had not lost the tanks and the trained Panzertruppen at Mailly-le-Camp, that first day on the beaches and, indeed, the whole Normandy campaign, might not have gone so well. It is worth remembering that the Allied losses on D-Day, 6 June 1944, were less than 2,500 men, of whom 1,000 died on "Omaha" beach. By way of comparison, on the first day of the battle of the Somme in 1916, 21,000 Allied soldiers lost their lives.

Although the 97 Squadron crew in which Frank Broughton was the wireless operator emerged from the attack physically unscathed, their new pilot may have suffered a trauma of which no-one knew but he. He captained the crew on three more operations - all to French targets, where the opposition caused no fearsome threat to life or limb - and then, on 22nd May, they set off

for Brunswick, but they never got that far: they only got close enough to see
the wall of searchlights and the flak barrage ahead. The pilot switched on his
microphone. "We're not flying through that," he said. "I'm turning back." The
navigator tried to dissuade him from that course of action, and so did the other
members of the crew. They spoke of the stigma of being classed as "LMF" -
lacking morale fibre - and of the shame that would be brought upon them all.
The pilot was unmoved: he was not going to fly through that barrage. They
returned to Coningsby and, by the next afternoon, the pilot had gone from the
squadron and out of their lives. The crew never saw him again, and that, in one
way, was a considerable misfortune: they stayed on at Coningsby, flying as
"spare bods" with any pilot who was short of a crewman for a while (it took
Broughton until VE-Day, working like that, to accomplish twenty-one
missions). For the pilot, it was tragedy. The establishments which dealt with
such cases as his, while less unpleasant in a physical sense than a prisoner-of-
war camp, were, in their effect on the spirit, on the *amour propre*, probably
more sapping. Eventually - and it could only have been at his own request - the
unhappy pilot returned to operations, with another squadron and a new crew. It
was their ill luck that the fates had not done with him: they all died together on
their first operation. It may be that those who died on 3/4 May were not the
only casualties of Mailly-le-Camp.

Then, there was the matter of the "third of an op" rule. Bert Garlick, the
12 Squadron air gunner, was asked, many years later, how he felt when he first
heard about that edict. His answer was succinct: "Sick."

"And after Mailly-le-Camp?"

"Positively ill."

The rule did not last long. On 10th May, eighty-nine aircraft of No. 5
Group attacked a target in Lille, hardly twelve minutes flying time from the
Belgian coast, and experienced a similar delay to that which had cost No. 1
Group so dear a week before. The initial target indicators were extinguished by
bombs, and the aiming-point had to be re-marked. During the hiatus, twelve
bombers were shot down - a loss-rate of over 13 per cent. No more was heard
of the "third of an op" rule after that: every European operation, with effect
retrospectively, counted as a whole one.

A more immediate outcome of the Mailly-le-Camp experience was of a
technical nature: on the following day, the transmitter crystal of the Master
Bomber frequency in the VHF set of every main force aircraft was removed.
The heavy bomber captains would still hear their instructions but, from that
day on, they could not talk back.

Another event which has to be recorded is that the Special Duty Flight, which had provided the "1 Group Controller", did not long continue in that role: it was disbanded two months later, due to what were described as "outside pressures", and the surviving captains, crews and aircraft returned to the squadrons from which they had been drawn to serve their AOC's requirement.

Last in this analysis comes an anecdote which may serve to sum the story up. Denzil Ede, the 626 Squadron navigator of UM M-Mike Two, whose pilot had tried to call his friend in UM S-Sugar Two above the English Channel, was shot down with his crew over Aachen at the end of May. In the prisoner-of-war camps, there was a stock question the "Kriegies" asked of one another, to start a conversation which might while away the time. Ede's companion was a gnarled rear gunner, who had been shot down half-way through his second tour. Expecting a dissertation on the respective claims of Berlin, Nuremburg or the valley of the Ruhr, Ede put the question: "Which was your worst trip?"

The veteran answered without a moment's hesitation: "Mailly-le-Camp."

EPILOGUE

This has been the story of a battle - one among hundreds that were fought over Europe between the RAF's bombers and the Luftwaffe's night-fighters in the course of World War II. It was not a momentous, history-making battle - it lasted less than sixty minutes, and it cost no more than two-hundred and fifty lives on either side - but it was bitterly contested and ever-remembered by those who were engaged. Looked at dispassionately, its main interest lies in the effective diversion of the long-range bomber force to a tactical objective - effective, that is, if the use of a bulldozer to knock a house of cards down can be regarded in that light - and in the meticulous, if under- advertised, conception of the plan. Viewed less coldly, it becomes a human drama - a story of endeavour. Reading any such a tale, in which conflict is the theme, we want to identify the heroes and the villains, and at the end of it, we want to know who won. In the account of the air battle over Mailly-le-Camp, these needs are unfulfilled. No-one can say to whom the victory went: there were winners and losers in the camps of both combatants. And real life stories tend to break the rules: those cast as the heroes make horrible mistakes, and those who should be villains are someone else's heroes.

On the night of 3/4 May, there were many heroes: the sky was full of them, and there were others on the ground. There were the pilots who stayed at the controls while their crews escaped the aircraft; there were the air-gunners who manned their turrets to the last; there was Maurice Garlick, who suffered agonies rather than let himself be captured, conduct for which he was later rewarded with the Order of the British Empire; there were the people of France who aided him and many others at great risk to themselves. Among the bomber captains, one man, perhaps, stands out among the rest: the late Squadron Leader Sparks of 83 Squadron. That Ned Sparks received no decoration for his sterling efforts in the midst of all the carnage is yet another mystery in the story of that night. As for the villains, who were they? The night-fighter pilots? Laurence Deane's wireless-mechanic? The air staff planners? None really fits the bill. The night-fighter men were fighting for their country, right or wrong; the mechanic may have been incompetent, and that is not a sin; the planners made mistakes, but if that is villainy, how many of us would not have to be condemned? Mistakes and malfunctions are corollaries of war, and have to be expected in any operation; when several coincided with a three-quarter moon, it needed no villains to bring the heroes down.

Scores of French patriots, both men and women, put their lives in jeopardy to help the evaders, and only a handful have been named in this account. Of these, the fate of Marcel Doré, gallant slaughterman of Montmoret, has been recorded - recorded with sadness and with admiration. Madame Bertin of Soulaines-Dhuys took an increasingly active part in the Resistance until the Liberation, including an attempt to buy Sergeant Preece's release from Châlons-sur-Mer gaol (which might have been successful if he had still been there). She received many honours from the Allied powers, and retained the affection and gratitude of all whom she had aided. In her late seventies, she died in 1980. Her son and daughter maintain their contact with the surviving evaders, and they meet now and then at the graves in la Ville-aux-Bois where, as children, they laid their tricolour bouquets. The moving spirit behind their meetings was Jim Carpenter, who could not forget that, had it not been for the toss of a coin, it might have been his bones that lay in la Ville-aux-Bois.

Joseph Lebrun, the brave rural postman, moved away from Estissac and now lives on the outskirts of Paris, as do his daughters and his son, who was born soon after the time of liberation, and whom the Lebruns called Maurice after a certain RAF navigator they had come to know. Of Lebrun, the words can be left to those who knew him best. "No, he didn't strike one as a heroic type," said the present deputy mayor of Estissac. "He was dark, short - a wiry sort of man. But he was a credit to France. He ran great risks, you understand. And his children never uttered a word, not even to the neighbours. If they had, he would have been a dead man." Charles Decreon, the farmer, also has a view of Joe Lebrun: "He was a little man, you know, but brave with it. He was arrested four times: once, the gendarmes stopped him and asked him what was in the car. "If you really want to know, I have four Indians," he said, and opened the rear door. Four American airmen were there. "You see, Indian farm-workers." said Lebrun, laughing, and slapped a gendarme on the back. A little cheek does wonders sometimes. The gendarme closed the door. "On your way," he said. "We haven't seen them.""

In 1991, Decreon was living quietly in Bucey, and the land was managed by his son. At the age of eighty-four, he was still a handsome man, and his faculties were excellent, although he was no longer strong. He was proud of his citations from Supreme Headquarters, signed by General Dwight D. Eisenhower, and from the Royal Air Force, signed by Air Chief Marshal Sir Arthur Tedder. Listening to his memories, you could sense the blend of humour and courage which served him so well - and those who relied on him - throughout those dreadful years.

"The last ones to leave here," he said, "were the SS. They shot at everything in the fields. They shot a woman picking dandelions for her pet rabbits. I still had certain missions at that time, riding on my motor-bike. An SS man jumped into the road in front of me with a machine-gun. "Your papers," he said. I laughed. "Did I frighten you?" I asked him. "A German soldier is never afraid." "Never afraid? Get on my bike and give me the gun, you'll see!" "Your papers."

At the time they were blowing up their blockhouses. I pretended not to know: "What is it," I said, "sabotage?"

"No," he said, "we're leaving."

"What's the difference? You leave, there'll be others." Then, for some reason, I let out: "I'm sick to death of the war."

"Me too," he said. I tell you, it made me feel better to hear an SS man say that."

Mike Allen, the bomb-aimer in 1st Lieutenant Dawley's 12 Squadron "jinx" crew, writing to me recently, confided his thoughts of 1944. He had met a "Georgia peach" while under training in the Southern States, attempting - and, like many others, failing - to become a pilot, and had returned there to find her when the war was won. That mission was abortive, and he had made a westward diversion to the state where "the corn is as high as an elephant's eye" - something he had wanted to do ever since Lail Dawley had made him listen to the songs from 'Oklahoma'. There, he met and married an "Okie," with whom he eventually set up home in Texas. It was from Houston that he wrote.

"At this late stage in life, one wonders at the psychological techniques one used to get through that period. We were lucky to be so young and indestructible. After our last op, the ground crew told us that they never once doubted our safe return, whereas they had often had accurate forebodings about other crews.

Later, I was to learn the importance of PMA - a positive mental attitude, which was what Dawley instilled in us, and what Churchill instilled in the British people."

And so to the questions which, while writing the story, have often come to mind: "What would my mental attitude have been, over that assembly point? How would I have liked it, orbiting a marker for fifteen minutes in the moonlight among the rest of 1 Group and a pack of night-fighters?" The answer to the questions never changed - I would not have liked it. I would have complained. Not with the transmit button pressed - RT discipline, as opposed to any other kind, was strict within the crew - but on the intercom. The response would probably have been "Aw, dry yer eyes, Skip", and the navigator would have asked to know of any change in airspeed, height or course (Mike Allen would have approved his PMA). The others would have sat and suffered as usual, with all antennae twitching, hoping for the best. There wasn't much else that anyone could do. It would have been another case of flying the aeroplane as defensively as possible, and trusting Lady Luck.

That is clearly what most people did over the assembly-point north of Mailly-le-Camp. Some of them - too many - ran out of luck; others showed frustration, a few voiced their alarm, and they should not have done that, but who am I to blame them? They should not have had the cause. There were many among them who, five weeks earlier, had lived through the slaughter of the Nuremberg raid, and were understandably reluctant to repeat the experience.

What has to be remembered about Mailly-le-Camp is that, with all hell bubbling up around them, and their fabric of existence hanging by a thread, the great majority of captains and crews gritted their teeth and waited for the order. In that, they won a greater battle than the one they had been briefed for. And when, at last, they were allowed to turn their sights towards the target, there were no more malfunctions and no more mistakes. Then, the bomber crews kept faith with their tradition, and with their comrades - with the fifty-five thousand who had died or were to die in other battles, and with those who would fly on until the war was won.

Mailly-le-Camp Association, France

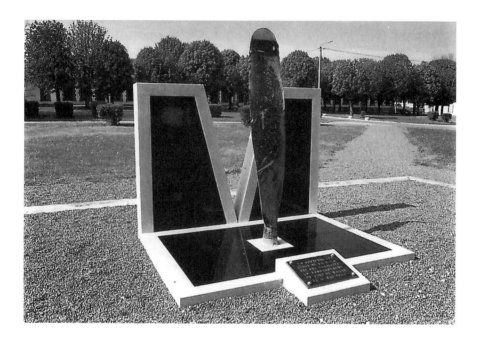

Founded at the beginning of 1990, originally as a committee to organise a ceremony in collaboration with the servicemen of Mailly-le-Camp, the Association has erected a stele to honour those airmen who took part in the operation.

A propellor blade from an allied bomber which crashed in the area was reclaimed, and forms the principal element of the monument, which includes a plaque paying tribute to those whose lives were sacrificed in the struggle for the liberation of France.

Further information on this Association may be obtained from the publishers.

GLOSSARY

AOC	Air Officer Commanding.
B17	Boeing 'Flying Fortress' Bomber.
Chance light	A powerful mobile light deployed at the down-wind end of the runway to assist take-off and landing.
C-in-C	Air Officer Commanding-in-Chief.
'Elint'	Electronic intelligence.
'Frying-Pan'	Aircraft dispersal hard-standing.
'Gee'	Air navigation aid. Three ground stations radiate pulses which appear on an instrument in the aircraft; the measured difference in their arrival time, when related to a special chart, gives the aircraft's position.
Geschwader	Luftwaffe formation deploying 100 to 200 aircraft, and comprising three or four Gruppen (q.v.).
Gruppe	Luftwaffe formation approximating to an RAF squadron, comprising three or four Staffeln (q.v.), and a Staab (Staff) flight.
Hauptmann	Rank equivalent to Flight Lieutenant.
'Mae West'	Inflatable life-jacket worn by aircrews.
Nachtjagdgeschwader	Luftwaffe night-fighter formation.
'Oboe'	RAF blind-bombing aid, based on signals transmitted from two ground stations which define the aircraft's bomb release-point.
RCM	Radio counter-measures.
RT	Radio telephony.
'Screening'	Posting of aircrew to non-operational flying duties.
Staffel	Luftwaffe equivalent of an RAF flight, usually with nine aircraft.
Unteroffizier	Non-commissioned officer.
USAAF	United States Army Air Force.
'Vic'	Standard RAF V-shaped flying formation of three aircraft.
'Wilde Sau'	Literally: 'Wild Sow'. Luftwaffe day-fighter operating in a night-fighter role.
WT	Wireless telegraphy.
'Zahme Sau'	Literally: 'Tame Sow': Luftwaffe radio-controlled night-fighter.

APPENDIX

RAF Losses

Lancaster BIII	JB405	Code letters PH+H
12 Squadron, 1 Group		
Crash Site:	Beauchery (Seine et Marne)	
Crew:	7 killed, 1 taken prisoner	
Pilot:	Plt. Off. John Dennis Carter, 21	
Navigator:	Flg. Off. Raymond John Ward, 24	
Wireless Operator:	Sgt. Geoffrey Long, 22	
Flight Engineer:	Sgt. Thomas Stanley Hayhurst, 30	
Bomb Aimer:	Sgt. Kenneth Norman Read, 22	
Mid Upper Gunner:	Sgt. Alexander Paton Simpson	
Rear Gunner:	Sgt. Septimus Johnson. Taken prisoner	
Copilot:	W.O. Douglas Eston Close (RAAF), 22	

All the dead were buried in the Beauchery communal cemetery, with the crew of Lancaster ND411 of 103 squadron, which crashed in the same area.

Lancaster BIII	JB748	Code letters PH+Z
12 Squadron, 1 Group		
Crash Site:	Courtisols (Marne)	
Crew:	7 killed	
Pilot:	Flg. Off. James Henry Ormrod, 21	
Navigator:	Flt. Sgt. Eric Stanley Hutchinson, 20	
Wireless Operator:	Sgt. Mark Thomas Wheeler	
Flight Engineer:	Sgt. John James Read	
Bomb Aimer:	Flg. Off. Hugh William Vaughan Bearne, 22	
Mid Upper Gunner:	Sgt. James Leslie Bradburn	
Rear Gunner:	Sgt. Leslie Johnson	

This aircraft crashed to the west of Courtisols. The crew were buried in the communal cemetery, together with the crew of the other Lancaster.

Lancaster BIII   LM514   Code letters PH+Q
12 Squadron, 1 Group
Crash Site: Close to the 'Belle-Idée' farm, 4 kilometres south
of Arcis-sur-Aube (near the village of St-Etienne-sous-Barbuise, Aube)
Crew: 1 taken prisoner, 6 escaped
Pilot: Flg. Off. Peter G Maxwell, escaped
Navigator: Flg. Off. Maurice Garlick, escaped
Wireless Operator: Sgt. Harold Lloyd, taken prisoner
Flight Engineer: Sgt. John Crighton, escaped
Bomb Aimer: Flt. Sgt. Herbert F. O'Hara, escaped
Mid Upper Gunner: Sgt. James Davidson, escaped
Rear Gunner: Sgt. Ernest (Bert) Townsend, escaped

The aircraft probably fell close to the 'Belle-Idée' farm at the village of St
Etienne-sous-Barbuise, on the RN77, with no fatalities amongst its crew,
although Sgt. Davidson, later injured whilst handling a weapon, died at the
Hôtel 'Dieu de Troyes' on May 26th.

Lancaster BIII   LM516   Code letters PH+D
12 Squadron, 1 Group
Crash Site: Mailly le Camp/Poivres (Aube)
Crew: 7 killed
Pilot: W.O. Sydney William Payne, 23
Navigator: Flt. Sgt. George Hogg
Wireless Operator: Flt. Sgt. William Alfred Harris, 23
Flight Engineer: Sgt. James Oldfields, 23
Bomb Aimer: Flt. Sgt. Ian Forbes Stuart, 24
Mid Upper Gunner: W.O. Claude William Croft, 22
Rear Gunner: Sgt. John Berry, 24

All these men were buried at the Poivres cemetery (Aube)

Lancaster BIII   DV275   Code letters SR+X2
101 Squadron, 1 Group
Crash Site: Mailly le Camp/Poivres (Aube)
Crew: 8 killed
Pilot: Plt. Off. George Baker
Navigator: Flt. Sgt. (or Flg. Off.) John Edwin Steward, 21
Wireless Operator: W.O. Donald Hubert McNaught (RAAF), 21
Flight Engineer: Sgt. David Harry Cro, 20
Bomb Aimer: Flt. Sgt. Sydney Wilson Ainsworth
Mid Upper Gunner: Flt. Sgt. Michael John Hackett (RAAF), 20
Rear Gunner: Sgt. Arthur John Ridgeway, 20
Special Duties Operator: Flg. Off. George Alexander Blair, 21

All these men were buried at the Poivres cemetery (Aube)

Lancaster BIII   LM417   Code letters SR+A
101 Squadron, 1 Group
Crash Site: Dravegny, Aisne
Crew: 7 killed, 1 taken prisoner
Pilot: Plt. Off. T. J. Drew
Navigator: Flg. Off. I. M. Bremner
Wireless Operator: Sgt. C. G. Dudley
Flight Engineer: Sgt. S. J. Rodway
Bomb Aimer: Sgt. H. N. Merrion, taken prisoner
Mid Upper Gunner: Sgt. F. G. Walter
Rear Gunner: Sgt. J. M. Davies
Special Duties Operator: Flt.Sgt. W. R. Walker

The dead were buried at the Dravegny cemetery.

Lancaster BIII   LM467   Code letters SR+J
101 Squadron, 1 Group
Crash Site: Voué (Aube)
Crew: 8 killed
Pilot: Flg. Off. Kenneth William Angus Muir, 22
Navigator: Flt. Sgt. Nigel Arthur Lacey-Johnson, 23
Wireless Operator: Sgt. John Gregory Woods
Flight Engineer: Sgt. James Bailey, 19
Bomb Aimer: Sgt. Norman Reginald Bishop, 20
Mid Upper Gunner: Sgt. Eric Edward Borton
Rear Gunner: Sgt. Arthur James Bowles, 19
Special Duties Operator: Plt. Off. John Joseph Gorman, 25

All these men were buried at the Voué cemetery.

Lancaster BI   ME564   Code letters SR+Z
101 Squadron, 1 Group
Crash Site: Aubeterre (Aube)
Crew: 7 killed, 1 taken prisoner
Pilot: F/L J. A. Keard
Navigator: Flg. Off. A. M. Shannon (RCAF)
Wireless Operator: Sgt. R. J. Crawford
Flight Engineer: Sgt. R. Webster
Bomb Aimer: Sgt. R. J. Spowart
Mid Upper Gunner: Sgt. A. Clarence
Rear Gunner: Sgt. J. E. Worsfold, taken prisoner
Wireless Operator / Special Operator: Plt. Off. D. C. Frazer

Seven crew members were buried at Aubeterre, and later re-buried in the
military cemetery at Hautot-sur-Mer near Dieppe (Seine Maritime).

Lancaster BIII   ND860   Code letter J
Special Duties Flight, 1 Group
Crash Site: St Rémy-sous-Barbuise (Aube)
Crew: 7 killed
Pilot: F/L William Edgar Hull, DFC, 21
Navigator: Flg. Off. Ronald Douglas Wilson, DFM, 26
Wireless Operator: Plt. Off. Cyril Atkinson (Reed), 27
Flight Engineer: Flt. Sgt. Frederick Joseph Bell, 28
Bomb Aimer: Flg. Off. William Widger, DFM
Air Gunner: Flt. Sgt. Eric Bailey, 23
Air Gunner: Flt. Sgt. James Charles Earl, DFM

This aircraft crashed near the village of St Rémy-sous-Barbuise and the crew
were buried in the local cemetery with some of the crew of Lancaster JA901-
which crashed at Droupt-Ste-Marie - and the crew of DV281.

Lancaster BI   ME673   Code letters PM+I
103 Squadron, 1 Group
Crash Site: Châlons-sur-Marne (Marne)
Crew: 7 killed
Pilot: Plt. Off. Sydney Lawrence Rowe, 28
Navigator: Flt. Sgt. Ernest George Housden, 23
Wireless Operator: Sgt. Kenneth Robert Warren, 22
Flight Engineer: Sgt. Jack Henry Sallis
Bomb Aimer: Flt. Sgt. Edward Arthur Metcalfe, 22
Air Gunner: Sgt. Phillip Arthur Staniland, 19
Air Gunner: Sgt. Dennis John Coldicott, 21

The aircraft crashed at Saint-Memmie at a place called 'Fonteney', causing the
death of two children and leaving 23 people injured. The explosion blew out
all the window panes in the vicinity, including those of the Châlons-sur-Marne
hospital 700 metres away. The bodies of five of the crew were found close to
the wreckage of the aircraft.
All the crew were buried in the community cemetery.

Lancaster BIII	ND411	Code letters PM+J

103 Squadron, 1 Group

Crash Site:	Beauchery (Seine et Marne)
Crew:	7 killed
Pilot:	Plt. Off. John Edgar Holden, 20
Navigator:	Sgt. Terence William Sykes, 20
Wireless Operator:	Sgt. Robert Arthur Wilson
Flight Engineer:	Sgt. James Ernest Moore
Bomb Aimer:	Flt. Sgt. Clifford Samuel Gay (RAAF), 27
Air Gunner:	Sgt. Arthur Arnold McCallum (RCAF)
Air Gunner:	Sgt. Fred Carson Hoxford (RCAF)

Hit by a night fighter, the aircraft crashed on the land of the village of Beauchery. The crew were buried along with those of Lancaster JB405 of 12 Squadron, which crashed close by.

Lancaster BIII	ND905	Code letters PM+B

103 Squadron, 1 Group

Crash Site:	Villers-le-Château (Marne)
Crew:	7 killed
Pilot:	Squadron Leader Harold Swanston, 32
Navigator:	Flg. Off. Eric John Dane, 23
Wireless Operator:	W.O. John Coates Smith, 23
Flight Engineer:	Sgt. Dennis Allen Hadden, 22
Bomb Aimer:	W.O. Ronald Howard Boyd (RAAF), 32
Air Gunner:	Sgt. George Francis Casey (RCAF), 32
Air Gunner:	Sgt. Jack Raymond Rankin (RCAF)

This aircraft was, in all likelihood, attacked by a night fighter near Châlons-sur-Marne and it crashed in the area of Villers-le-Château.

Lancaster BI   LL743   Code letters AS+U
166 Squadron, 1 Group
Crash Site: Chapelle-Vallon (Aube)
Crew: 2 killed, 4 taken prisoner, 1 escaped
Pilot: Flt. Sgt. John A. Sanderson (RNZAF), taken
prisoner
Navigator: Sgt. R. G. Marks, taken prisoner
Wireless Operator: Sgt. W. T. Violett, escaped
Flight Engineer: Sgt. F. J. Solomon, taken prisoner
Bomb Aimer: Sgt. C. Farley, taken prisoner
Mid Upper Gunner: Sgt. John Thomas Cockburn, 21, killed
Rear Gunner: Sgt. Jack Arthur Bodsworth, 27, killed

Sgts. Cockburn and Bodsworth were buried at the cemeteries of Chapelle-
Vallon and Voué respectively.

Lancaster BI   ME643   Code letters AS+E
166 Squadron, 1 Group
Crash Site: Courtisols (Marne)
Crew: 7 killed
Pilot: Plt. Off. William Mornington Edmund Myers
Navigator: Flt. Sgt. Stanley Wilson, 21
Wireless Operator: Flt. Sgt. William Thomas Jones, 20
Flight Engineer: Sgt. Robert Alfred Green, 20
Bomb Aimer: Plt. Off. Anthony Peter Pappajohn (RCAF)
Mid Upper Gunner: Sgt. Joseph Patrick Kenny, 31
Rear Gunner: Sgt. Ronald Frank Arnold

This aircraft crashed in the area of Courtisols with no survivors. The crew
were buried at the local cemetery with the crew of JB748.

Lancaster BI   ME749   Code letters AS+Z
166 Squadron, 1 Group
Crash Site: St-Maurice-aux-Riches-Hommes (Yonne)
Crew: 1 killed, 3 taken prisoner, 3 escaped
Pilot: Plt. Off. G. T. A. Harrison (RAAF) escaped
Navigator: Sgt. R. W. Watson (RAAF) escaped
Wireless Operator: Sgt. R. H. Haynes, escaped
Flight Engineer: Sgt. J. Marsden, taken prisoner
Bomb Aimer: Sgt. E. W. J. Ashford, taken prisoner
Mid Upper Gunner: Flg. Off. G. V. O'Brien (RAAF) taken prisoner
Rear Gunner: Sgt. Henry Pickford, 19, killed

The aircraft crashed near the Chaume, in the area of St-Maurice. Sgt. Pickford
was buried in the local cemetery. His body was exhumed and taken to the
Terlinetum British Cemetery at Wimille (Pas-de-Calais) on the 4th December
1972.

Lancaster BIII   JB741   Code letters AR+J
460 Squadron RAAF, 1 Group
Crash Site: Dommartin-Lettrée (Marne)
Crew: 7 killed
Pilot: Plt. Off. Francis William Baker
Navigator: Plt. Off. (or Sgt.) Willis Henry Thompson (RCAF),
27
Wireless Operator: Sgt. George Edward O'Neill (RAF)
Flight Engineer: Sgt. James William Ranger (RAF), 19
Bomb Aimer: Flt. Sgt. Wilfred Bernard Martin (RCAF), 23
Air Gunner: Sgt. William Cochrane Maxwell (RAF), 21
Air Gunner: Sgt. Harry Penrice Black (RAF), 19

The crew were all buried at the Dommartin-Lettrée cemetery

Lancaster BI   ME728   Code letters AR+Z2
460 Squadron RAAF, 1 Group
Crash Site: Avant-les-Marcilly (Aube)
Crew: 7 killed
Pilot: Plt. Off. Norman David Livingston Lloyd, 30
Navigator: Flt. Sgt. Ronald Henry Hobbs, 20
Wireless Operator: Flt. Sgt. Dennis Ronald Barr, 20
Flight Engineer: Sgt. John George Turnbull (RAF), 24
Bomb Aimer: Flt. Sgt. Brian Thomas Wootton-Woolley (RAF)
Air Gunner: Sgt. Peter Dennis Fry (RAF), 20
Air Gunner: Sgt. Richard Anthony Johnson (RAF), 22

The aircraft crashed at the eastern entrance to the village of Avant-les-Marcilly, a few metres from the first houses. All the crew were found dead at the scene and were buried in the cemetery around the church.

Lancaster BI   ME740   Code letters AR+E
460 Squadron RAAF, 1 Group
Crash Site: Marigny-le-Grand (Marne)
Crew: 7 killed
Pilot: Flt. Sgt. Herbert James George Fry, 26
Navigator: Flg. Off. Leslie Sumner (RAF), 30
Wireless Operator: Sgt. Kenneth Applegarth (RAF), 20
Flight Engineer: Sgt. Joseph Horace Holloway (RAF), 28
Bomb Aimer: Flt. Sgt. William Ralph Elgar, 23
Air Gunner: Plt. Off. (or Sgt.) Thomas Sudworth Winstanley
(RCAF), 22
Air Gunner: Sgt. Cecil George Graham (RAF)

All the crew perished and were buried in the local cemetery.

Lancaster BIII	LM531	Code letters AR+R

460 Squadron RAAF, 1 Group

Crash Site:	Châlons sur Marne (Marne)
Crew:	4 killed, 3 escaped
Pilot:	W.O. George Kenneth Gritty (RAF), 29
Navigator:	Sgt. Joseph Orbin, escaped
Wireless Operator:	Sgt. Stanley Roland Russell (RAF), 22
Flight Engineer:	Sgt. Lionel Robert Vale (RAF), 19
Bomb Aimer:	Sgt. Léonard Henri Williams, escaped
Mid Upper Gunner:	Sgt. Joseph Chandler (RAF), 21
Rear Gunner:	Flt. Sgt. Bryan Morgan, escaped, 20

The crew members who were killed were buried at the Châlons-sur-Marne cemetery with the crew of ME673 of 103 squadron which crashed the same night at Saint-Memmie.

The Lancaster came down at Châlons-sur-Marne in a garden between the streets 'Porte Murée' and 'Mélinet', causing a fire in the home of Mademoiselle Potlet. Several people were injured by the falling wreckage. The bodies of the dead airmen were found in the debris in Rue Mélinet.

Lancaster BIII	ND630	Code letters AR+G

460 Squadron RAAF, 1 Group

Crash Site:	Chapelle-Vallon (Aube)
Crew:	7 killed
Pilot:	Plt. Off. Joseph William Smart, 21
Navigator:	Flt. Sgt. George Charles Barber, 32
Wireless Operator:	Sgt. Francis Findley Naismith (RAF), 21
Flight Engineer:	Sgt. Thomas Oulton (RAF), 19
Bomb Aimer:	Plt. Off. George Robert Warnock (RCAF), 26
Air Gunner:	Plt. Off. Arthur Bryson Moore (RCAF)
Air Gunner:	Flt. Sgt. Ernest Frederick Stannett (RAF), 24

This aircraft crashed in the area of Chapelle-Vallon. None of the crew survived, and they were buried in the local cemetery together with Sgt. Cockburn, the sole fatality from Lancaster LL743 of 166 squadron, which crashed nearby.

Lancaster BI   LL826   Code letters BQ+H
550 Squadron RAF, 1 Group
Crash Site: Cheniers (Marne)
Crew: 8 killed
Pilot: F/L Arthur James Grain DFM
Navigator: Flg. Off. Melvin Robert Oliver (RCAF), 24
Wireless Operator: Flg. Off. Harold Weston Batt, 32
Flight Engineer: Sgt. John Stanley, 21
Bomb Aimer: Flg. Off. Edward Crowther Jones (RCAF), 23
Air Gunner: Sgt. James Ellis, 36
Air Gunner: Sgt. Kenneth Reginald Dye, 19
Passenger: Major Sidney Whipp, The Duke of Wellington's
Regiment, Station Defence Officer

All the crew were buried at the Cheniers cemetery.

Lancaster BI   ME586   Code letters UL+B2
576 Squadron RAF, 1 Group
Crash Site: Oeuilly (Marne)
Crew: 5 killed, 2 taken prisoner
Pilot: Plt. Off. Roy Whalley, DFC, 22
Navigator: Sgt. J. D. Ward, taken prisoner
Wireless Operator: Flt. Sgt. Fred Burgess, 23
Flight Engineer: Sgt. C. Vandevelde, taken prisoner
Bomb Aimer: Flt. Sgt. Stanley James Barr, 22
Air Gunner: Sgt. Jeremiah McCool, 26
Air Gunner: Flt. Sgt. Norman Parry Reilly, 21

The five dead were buried at Oeuilly.

Lancaster BIII   LM317   Code letters CF+U
625 Squadron, 1 Group
Crash Site: Mailly-le-Camp/Poivres (Aube)
Crew: 7 killed
Pilot: Plt. Off. Charles David Angelo Short
Navigator: Flg. Off. Robert Edward Haddock, 26
Wireless Operator: Sgt. James Francis Moran, 23
Flight Engineer: Sgt. John Albert Williams
Bomb Aimer: W.O. II (or Flt. Sgt.) John Albert Reynolds
(RCAF), 20
Mid Upper Gunner: Sgt. Raymond Henri Martin, 35
Rear Gunner: Flt. Sgt. Neal Earl Parker (RAAF), 21

All these men are buried at the Poivres Cemetery.

Lancaster BIII   LM515   Code letters CF+W
625 Squadron, 1 Group
Crash Site: Trouan-le-Petit (Aube)
Crew: 7 killed
Pilot: Plt. Off. Neil McArthur McGaw
Navigator: Sgt. Frederick Charles Clarke, 23
Wireless Operator: Sgt. Reginald John Tailby, 23
Flight Engineer: Sgt. Kenneth Garner, 20
Bomb Aimer: Flg. Off. Daniel Moriarty (RCAF)
Mid Upper Gunner: Sgt. Richard Walter Andrews
Rear Gunner: Flt. Sgt. Thomas Charles White (RAAF), 20

The whole crew were buried at the Trouan-le-Petit cemetery.

Lancaster BI   ME697   Code letters CF+A
625 Squadron, 1 Group
Crash Site: St-Agnan (Yonne)
Crew: 5 killed, 1 taken prisoner, 1 escaped
Pilot: Squadron Leader R. W. H. Gray, taken prisoner
Navigator: Flg. Off. Leslie Frank Medway, 20, killed
Wireless Operator: Sgt. P. J. Evans, escaped
Flight Engineer: Flg. Off. David Charles Martin, 28, killed
Bomb Aimer: Flt. Sgt. Walter Alec Clarence Footman, 24, killed
Mid Upper Gunner: Plt. Off. John George Johnson (RCAF), 31, killed
Rear Gunner: Sgt. Benjamin Escritt, 23, killed

The five dead were buried at the local cemetery.

Lancaster BI   DV281   Code letters UM+D2
626 Squadron, 1 Group
Crash Site: St Rémy sous Barbuise (Aube)
Crew: 7 killed
Pilot: Flt. Sgt. Percy James William Barkway (RCAF)
Navigator: W.O. Ronald Duncan Weller (RCAF)
Wireless Operator: Sgt. John William Hooper, 21
Flight Engineer: Sgt. Frederick William Burton, 22
Bomb Aimer: Sgt. George Alfred Coote
Mid Upper Gunner: Sgt. (or Plt. Off.) Otto Molzan (RCAF)
Rear Gunner: Sgt. Russell Eugene Hogan, 20

The crew were buried at St Rémy-sous-Barbuise cemetery, next to the crew of
Lancaster ND860 of 101 squadron and the two fatalities from the crew of
Lancaster JA901 of 467 squadron, which crashed at Droupt-Ste-Marie.

<u>Lancaster BIII</u>   <u>EE148</u>   <u>Code letters UM+S2</u>
626 Squadron, 1 Group
Crash Site: Montigny-le-Guesdier (Seine et Marne)
Crew: 7 killed
Pilot: Plt. Off. Norman James Fisher, 29
Navigator: Sgt. Noel Hatton, 21
Wireless Operator: Sgt. Victor Ronald Roper, 22
Flight Engineer: Sgt. John Waites
Bomb Aimer: Flg. Off. Kenneth Thomas Larman, 21
Mid Upper Gunner: Sgt. Howard Measor Crooks, 19
Rear Gunner: Sgt. Robert Frederick Godfrey, 20

All the crew perished and were buried at the Montigny-le-Guesdier cemetery.

<u>Lancaster BI</u>   <u>LL753/G</u>   <u>Code letters UM+Z2</u>
626 Squadron, 1 Group
Crash Site: Breuvery-sur-Coole (Marne)
Crew: 7 killed
Pilot: Plt. Off. David Stuart Jackson, DFC, 21
Navigator: Plt. Off. Horace C. Riddle
Wireless Operator: Flt. Sgt. R. H. Walts
Flight Engineer: Sgt. A. I. Sutton
Bomb Aimer: W.O. J. M. B. Liebseher
Mid Upper Gunner: Sgt. A. J. Brooks
Rear Gunner: Plt. Off. (or Flt.Sgt.) Ross Edward MacFarlane
(RCAF)

Pilot Officers Jackson and MacFarlane were buried at the Breuvery-sur-Coole cemetery. The others have no known graves, but are recorded at Runnymede Memorial.

Lancaster BI   LL787   Code letters WS+Y
9 Squadron, 5 Group
Crash Site: Normée (Marne)
Crew: 5 killed, 1 escaped, 1 taken prisoner
Pilot: Flg. Off. James Frank Ineson, 22
Navigator: Plt. Off. Hugh Fraser MacKenzie (RCAF), 21
Wireless Operator: Sgt. Henry Robert Warren
Flight Engineer: Plt. Off. Leonard Charles Margetts, 29
Bomb Aimer: Flg. Off. T. L. N. Porteous, taken prisoner
Mid Upper Gunner: Sgt. H. S. Chappell, escaped
Rear Gunner: Sgt. James Wilkinson

The dead were buried at the Normée cemetery.

Lancaster BIII   EE185   Code letters KM+A
44 Squadron, 5 Group
Crash Site: In the area of Dreux (Eure and Loir)
Crew: 7 killed
Pilot: Plt. Off. A. W. Nolan
Navigator: Flt. Sgt. K. B. Milton
Wireless Operator: Sgt. J. C. Boreham
Flight Engineer: Sgt. Eric H. Charlton
Bomb Aimer: Plt. Off. E. G. Blake
Mid Upper Gunner: Sgt. R. D. Crook
Rear Gunner: Sgt. Patrick Higgins

The crew were buried at Dreux cemetery (Eure-et-Loir).

Lancaster BIII   ED870   Code letters VN+I
50 Squadron, 5 Group
Crash Site: Mailly-le-Camp/Poivres (Aube)
Crew: 8 killed
Pilot: Plt. Off. Albert Handley, 28
Navigator: Flg. Off. Theodore Edward Archard, 32
Wireless Operator: Sgt. Cyril Whitelock, 22
Flight Engineer: Sgt. Charles Thomas Brown
Bomb Aimer: Flt. Sgt. Robert Stanley Garrod, 22
Mid Upper Gunner: Sgt. David Bissett, 22
Rear Gunner: Sgt. George Edward Gilpin
Mid Under Gunner: Flt. Sgt. James Walker White (RCAF), 20

The crew were buried at Poivres cemetery.

Lancaster BIII   LM437   Code letters VN+P
50 Squadron, 5 Group
Crash Site: Trouan-le-Petit (Aube)
Crew: 6 killed, 1 escaped
Pilot: Plt. Off. Ronald Stanley Hanson, 22
Navigator: Flg. Off. William John Hopkins Rogers, 24
Wireless Operator: Sgt. W. Richardson, escaped
Flight Engineer: Sgt. Robert Alexander Sneddon
Bomb Aimer: W.O. II (or Flt. Sgt.) Gordon Herbert Hobson
(RCAF)
Mid Upper Gunner: Sgt. Eric Houlden (RCAF), 19
Rear Gunner: Sgt. Robert Mathew David

The six dead were buried at Trouan-le-Petit, together the dead of Lancaster
LM515 of 625 squadron, which also crashed in the area.

Lancaster BIII	LM480	Code letters VN+U
50 Squadron, 5 Group		
Crash Site:	St-Mesmin (Aube)	
Crew:	6 killed, 2 escaped	
Pilot:	F/L Thomas H Blackham, DFC, escaped	
Navigator:	Flg. Off. David Gwynfor Jones, 24	
Wireless Operator:	Sgt. Sidney Charles Wilkins, 21	
Flight Engineer:	Plt. Off. Charles Richard Ernest Walton, 28	
Bomb Aimer:	Flt. Sgt. Stanley J Godfrey, escaped	
Mid Upper Gunner:	Sgt. Herbert George Ridd, 29	
Rear Gunner:	Sgt. William Dennis Dixon, 20	
Co Pilot:	Plt. Off. Cyril Edward Stehensen	

A German night fighter attacked the aircraft over the target area. The Lancaster exploded and crashed at St-Mesmin, west of the RN19. The 5 dead were buried in the local cemetery.

Lancaster BIII	ND953	Code letters VN+S
50 Squadron, 5 Group		
Crash Site:	Lucy le Bocage (Aisne)	
Crew:	4 killed, 1 taken prisoner, 2 escaped	
Pilot:	Plt. Off. W. F. Dobson, escaped	
Navigator:	Flt. Sgt. D. R. Jefferies, taken prisoner	
Wireless Operator:	Sgt. F. Glover	
Flight Engineer:	Sgt. G. R. Williamson, escaped	
Bomb Aimer:	Sgt. G. W. Evans	
Air Gunner:	Sgt. Herbert George Ridd, 29	
Tail Gunner:	Sgt. J. W. Shaw	

The four crew members killed were buried at Marigny-en-Orxois cemetery (Ainse).

Lancaster BIII   <u>ND460</u>   <u>Code letters DX+M</u>
57 Squadron, 5 Group
Crash Site: The Vaudoué (Seine and Marne)
Crew: 7 killed
Pilot: Flg. Off. Rendal Anthony Fenwick Scrivener, 20
Navigator: Flg. Off. Norman Alfred Smith, 26
Wireless Operator: Sgt. Frederick Charles Searle, 21
Flight Engineer: Sgt. George Henry Norton, 21
Bomb Aimer: Flt. Sgt. Henry Mitchell Peckett, 20
Mid Upper Gunner: Flt. Sgt. Thomas Roy Clayton, 23
Rear Gunner: Flt. Sgt. James Kenneth Morey, 22

Hit by a night fighter south west of Melun, the bomber crashed close to the village of Vaudoué, where the crew are buried.

Lancaster BIII   <u>JB402</u>   <u>Code letters OL+R</u>
83 Squadron, 5 Group
Crash Site: Orbais-l'Abbaye (Marne)
Crew: 2 taken prisoner, 6 escaped
Pilot: Squadron Leader E. N. M. Sparks
Navigator: Plt. Off. J A Kraemer, taken prisoner
Wireless Operator: W.O. Donald A Woodland
Flight Engineer: Sgt. Cyril Steele
Bomb Aimer: F/L Lawson George Foley
Mid Upper Gunner: Flt. Sgt. Kenneth Hunter
2nd Navigator: F/L J W Tindall DFM

Lancaster BIII	ND706	Code letters OF+A
97 Squadron, 5 Group		
Crash Site:	(Yvelines)	
Crew:	7 killed	
Pilot:	Flg. Off. R. O. Ellesmere	
Navigator:	Plt. Off. S. Carlyle, DFM	
Wireless Operator:	Sgt. L. F. Hughes	
Flight Engineer:	Sgt. M. Johnson	
Bomb Aimer:	F/L A. E. Carlton	
Air Gunner:	Sgt. N. M. Duffy	
Air Gunner:	Plt. Off. A. J. Newton	

This aircraft crashed 3 kilometres south west of Allainville (6 kilometres from Dreux), where the crew were buried. The bodies were transferred after the war to the Lisieux-St-Désir cemetery (Calvados).

Lancaster BIII	ND515	Code letters EM+M
207 Squadron, 5 Group		
Crash Site:	Dontilly (Seine and Marne)	
Crew:	7 killed	
Pilot:	Plt. Off. Cyril Bell	
Navigator:	Flt. Sgt. Raymond Jack Cross, 26	
Wireless Operator:	Sgt. Raymond Barker, 22	
Flight Engineer:	Sgt. Raymond Ernest Dance, 18	
Bomb Aimer:	Plt. Off. (or Flt. Sgt.) Baskerville (RCAF), 24	
Air Gunner:	Plt. Off. Sidney Hulbert Willes	
Air Gunner:	Sgt. Howard Cullimore Jones	

This aircraft crashed near Donnemarie-Dontilly. All the crew perished and were buried in the Dontilly cemetery.

Lancaster BIII   ND556   Code letters EM+F
207 Squadron, 5 Group
Crash Site: Chaintreaux (Seine et Marne)
Crew: 2 killed, 1 taken prisoner, 4 escaped
Pilot: W.O. (or Flt. Sgt.) Leslie Harry Lissette (RNZAF),
26
Navigator: Flt. Sgt. J. Pittwood, escaped
Wireless Operator: Sgt. P. N. King, escaped
Flight Engineer: N. J. Stockford, escaped
Bomb Aimer: Sgt. L. Wesley, taken prisoner
Air Gunner: Sgt. R. T. Emeny, escaped
Air Gunner: Sgt. Ronald Ellis, 25

W.O. Lissette died from his injuries and was buried with his fellow crewman, Sgt. Ellis, at the Chaintreaux cemetery (Seine-et-Marne).

Lancaster BIII   LM458   Code letters JO+G
463 Squadron RAAF, 5 Group
Crash Site: Mailly-le-Camp/Poivre (Aube)
Crew: 7 killed
Pilot: Flg. Off. Graham Fryer, 24
Navigator: Flt. Sgt. John Bernard Ward, 21
Wireless Operator: Flt. Sgt. Edwin Andrew Stone, 21
Flight Engineer: Sgt. Robert Johnstone Gracey
Bomb Aimer: Flt. Sgt. Joseph Healy, 23
Mid Upper Gunner: Flg. Off. Henry Edward Williams, 25
Rear Gunner: Sgt. Kenneth William Owen

All these men were buried at the Poivres cemetery.

Lancaster BIII	JA901	Code letters PO+N

467 Squadron RAAF, 5 Group

Crash Site:	Droupt-Ste-Marie (Aube)
Crew:	5 killed, 2 escaped
Pilot:	Plt. Off. Colin Dickson, 23
Navigator:	Flt. Sgt. Oscar Skelton Furniss, 22
Wireless Operator:	Flt. Sgt. Robert Isaiah Hunter, escaped
Flight Engineer:	Sgt. Philip Joseph Weaver, 33
Bomb Aimer:	Flt. Sgt. Stanley D. Jolly, escaped
Mid Upper Gunner:	Sgt. Horace Skellorn, 19
Rear Gunner:	Flt. Sgt. Hilton Hardcastle Forden, 20

Five crewmen were found dead. Sgts. Forden and Skellorn were buried at St-Rémy-sous-Barbuise. Plt. Off. Dickson and Sgts. Furniss and Weaver were buried at Droupt-Ste-Marie. Their bodies were exhumed in March 1983 and placed in the military cemetery at Wimille (Pas de Calais).

Lancaster BIII	JB134	Code letters PG+G

617 Squadron, 5 Group

Crash Site:	Courboin (Aisne)
Crew:	8 killed
Pilot:	Plt. Off. D. Wadsworth, DFC
Navigator:	Flt. Sgt. A. C. Shenton
Wireless Operator:	Sgt. H. Brady, DFM
Flight Engineer:	Sgt. J. A. Burgess
Bomb Aimer:	Flt. Sgt. J. Bengston
Mid Upper Gunner:	Sgt. J. H. Maltby, DFM
Rear Gunner:	Sgt. F. H. Joy, DFM
2nd Air Bomber:	Sgt. O. Naylor

The crew were buried at the Couboin cemetery

Mosquito Mk II   <u>DD779</u>   <u>Code letters VI+</u>
169 Squadron, 100 Group
Crash Site: Champignol-lez-Mondeville (Aube)
Crew: 2 killed
Pilot: Plt. Off. Peter Lister Johnson
Navigator: Plt. Off. Mervyn Hopkins

This aircraft was on a electronics counter-measures mission (Serratte) - detecting the radar emissions of the German night fighters to protect the waves of bombers attacking Mailly. It crashed in a field near Champignol. The two crew were buried in the local cemetery.

Halifax MKIII   <u>MZ570</u>   <u>Code letters DT+V</u>
192 Squadron, 100 Group
Crash Site: Ville-au-Bois (Aube)
Crew: 2 killed, 2 escaped, 5 taken prisoner
Pilot: Flt. Sgt. H. R. Gibson, taken prisoner
Navigator: Sgt. Frank L. Preece, taken prisoner
Wireless Operator: Sgt. Frank Stormont, escaped
Flight Engineer: Sgt. John Oates Ackroyd, taken prisoner
Bomb Aimer: W.O. E. J. Elder, taken prisoner
Air Gunner: Sgt. Edward Cyril Cottrell, killed
Rear Gunner: Sgt. Albert William Burton, 35, killed
Air Gunner: Sgt. W. Nicholson, taken prisoner
Special Duties Operator: Flg. Off. Thomas W. Munro, escaped

During its patrol over the Aube countryside, MZ570 was attacked by an ME109. The aircraft exploded and crashed in the vicinity of Ville-au-Bois. Sgts. Cottrell and Burton were buried in the local cemetery.

BIBLIOGRAPHY

"Great Battle Tanks", Simon Dunstan, Ian Allan.

"Bomber Squadrons of the RAF", Philip Moyes, MacDonald & Jane's.

"Panzers at War", A.J.Barker, Ian Allan.

"Lancaster, the Story of a Famous Bomber", Bruce Robertson, Harleyford.

"The Strategic Air Offensive Against Germany 1939-45", Webster & Frankland, HMSO.

"Great Campaigns of World War II", J.B.Davies, Macdonald & Co.

"The Raid on Mailly-le-Camp", Bill Chorley, Aviation News, October 1986.

"Bomber Intelligence", W.E. Jones, Midland Counties Publications.

"Confound and Destroy", Martin Streetly, Macdonald & Jane's.

Richardson, Flight Sergeant • 59, 103, 181
Rilliot, Monsieur Mary • 135
Rommel, Generalfeldmarschall Erwin • 45, 122,
    128, 129, 131
Rundstedt, Generalfeldmarschall Gerd von • 122,
    131

S

Saint-Smith, Flying Officer J.A., DFC, DFM,
    RAAF • 63
Scarecrow flares • 83, 85, 91
Searby, Air Commodore John, DSO, DFC • 37
Shannon, Mrs. Ann • 105
Shannon, Squadron Leader David, DSO, DFC,
    RAAF • 30, 31, 39, 58, 61, 64, 66, 103, 147,
    154
Sherman, Lieutenant Bob, USAF • 119, 120
Skingley, Flying Officer J. • 72
Spark, Flying Officer J.R., DFM • 92, 100
Sparks, Squadron Leader R.N.M. • 50, 64, 66, 68,
    70, 72, 79, 81, 95, 105, 106, 120, 154, 160,
    183
Stephens, Flight Sergeant P., DFM • 51, 87
Stormont, Sergeant • 60, 109, 110, 119, 120, 137,
    187
Sumpter, Flight Lieutenant Len, DFC • 58, 61,
    66, 147, 151
Swaffield, Sergeant William R. • 92, 93

T

Tedder, Air Chiel Marshal Sir Arthur, GCB •
    128, 161
Thompson, Pilot Officer • 52, 173
Townsend, Sergeant Bert • 52, 126, 127, 133,
    137, 167

U

United States Army formations
    101st Airborne Division • 129
    1st Infantry Division • 129
    4th Infantry Division • 129
    5th Corps • 131
    7th Corps • 131
    82nd Airborne Division • 129

W

Warmington, Flying Officer W.I., DFC • 56, 79,
    85, 97, 130
Watson, Sergeant R.W. • 100, 173

Wayte, Flight Sergeant Louis, DFM • 78, 79, 146
Wehrmacht formations
    12th Panzer Division • 131
    15th Panzer Division • 45
    21st Panzer Division • 12, 45, 123, 131, 155
    91st Infantry Division • 123
    Panzer Lehr Division • 131
    Waffen SS Division • 45
Whipp, Major S., TD • 101, 176
Wilson, Flight Lieutenant George, DFC • 53, 86,
    146
Wittmann, Leutnant Michael • 47
Woodruff, Flying Officer Dick, DFM • 74, 85
Worsfold, Sergeant Jack • 108, 109, 169
Wright, Flight Lieutenant Tony, DFC • 54